Dear Marguerite:

With deepest gratitude I say "thank you" you put my story together perfectly! You put on paper what was in my heart. I'm hoping Cheryln can read my book, because it is partly her story as well.

Let's keep doing life big.

Ephessians 5:20
Philippians 4:6-9

"Do Life Big"
Virgil Christoffels

DO

LIFE

BIG

✂

PRAISE FOR
DO LIFE BIG

"*Do Life Big* is a fantastic game plan for making your dreams a reality and building an intentional legacy in the process. The message is clear, don't wait and don't settle—the best way to start is right now with this book!"

Tom Ziglar
CEO of Ziglar Inc.

"This book is an incredible work that will transform lives. I read every word and marked it with multiple color highlighters. Our lives are very similar and our paths, both spiritually and in business, run so many parallels. For anyone trying to pull the pieces of life together; from career, marriage, faith, wellness and all the other pieces that seem to not fit—this book, *Do Life Big*, has the roadmap you need. Virg has taken true life experiences and used them to map out a path to success that anyone at any age can use to connect the dots and build a successful life filled with balance, purpose, and priorities in place. From his love affair with God, his wife, and the building of a successful business through the lessons learned in good times and challenges, Virg gives the reader a compass that he calls a 'Life Success

Binder' to guide his readers toward starting to live life intentionally right now and to begin to 'Do Life Big'!" (Matthew 13:23, Ephesians 3:20–21).

Jeffrey Paul
Founder of Wigs For Kids, Owner of Hair & Scalp
Specialists, Author, and Inspirational Speaker

"*Do Life Big* will help anyone who reads and applies these simple practices to their life, live an extraordinary life so countless others will. Virg nails it."

John R. DiJulius, III
Bestselling Author of The Customer Service Revolution

"I had the pleasure of meeting Mr. Virg Christoffels at an International Convention in the autumn of 1982. From that day our relationship grew into a successful business and personal relationship even though we are almost 2,000 miles apart. Knowing Mr. Virg Christoffels that long, I assure you he possesses all the desired qualities of life, such as integrity, honesty, and hard work, as well as being a successful entrepreneur and a very happy family man. I believe one of his greatest strengths is his willingness to share his business acumen with others in order to help them be the success they want to be."

Andrew Wright
Founder and President of the largest
men's hair import company in the USA

"I've had the pleasure of knowing and working with Virg Christoffels and his team at Christoffels & Co. for many years as a supplier and educator. I was able to observe firsthand that Virg, powered by his faith, belief in people, and dedication to improving their lives, turned a job into a renowned career. His prescription of hard work, unbending ethics, and willingness to learn and change created more engaged employees, a constantly evolving business, and happier, more fulfilled customers. Virg has a worldview that says that when you care, people notice. His extraordinary business success is proof that those who possess skill, courage, integrity, decency, commitment, and generosity can create competitive immunity and can grow to become the industry gold standard. Virg has had a phenomenal impact!"

Lance Centofanti

Marketing Professional, Brand Developer, Industry Speaker

"For over twenty-five years, Christoffel's Hair Restoration has been a loyal and respected Hair Visions International™ business partner. In my tenure as president of Hair Visions™, I can't recall if I have experienced a more genuine businessperson than Virg Christoffels. As I interacted more with Virg over the past several years, I grew to value his expertise and business acumen more every day. His people and management skills are what have led to his phenomenal success. Virg became a key speaker at many Hair Visions'™ industry conferences, sharing his business strategies with other hair retailers. As Virg was planning his succession to his daughter, Sara, my team and I thought it would be hugely beneficial if Virg would consider sharing his vast knowledge of the hair industry with other retailers. In 2017, Hair Visions™ and Virg collaborated to create a training program offering training and coaching to other hair retailers worldwide. Due in great part to his people skills and knowledge of the industry, the program was a great success, and Virg's story resonated throughout the industry, creating more opportunity for others. I have the deepest respect and admiration for Virg for many reasons, including his compassion and courage."

David M. Schwartz

President, Hair Visions International™

"My friend Virg Christoffels is driven. He is also genuine. That's a tough combination. To be broad enough to focus on the big picture, yet small enough to notice the details! This book will cause you to examine your own story…if you're old enough to be looking back…and if you're young enough…to plan thoughtfully and effectively. There are lots of authors who tell you how…and very few who tell you why. Virg shares the reasons his life process has meaning. That's worth paying attention to.

Steve Garry

Friend, Garry Private Wealth Resources—Partner

"Anyone who knows Virg well knows that he does the right things… and he does things right. This is not by accident, but rather with great intention and attention.

Do Life Big is a wonderful book that honors the special relationship that he and Cheryln shared in life and in business, and inspires current or aspiring business owners to chart their own course to success. A profound and enjoyable read, this book is filled with practical tools and helpful advice. It will make you cry, make you laugh, and will help you develop a healthy perspective on what you want to achieve in business and in life!"

Dave Rozenboom
Friend, President, First PREMIER Bank

"Virg is a 'get it done' leader! He walks the talk. He is not the thunder; he is the rain—always delivers. As a trusted friend and accountability partner, we have walked side by side through the hard stuff, as well as sharing in one another's victories and celebrations.

The top priority for this entrepreneur is to glorify God in every detail of his journey. Virg demonstrates in his daily activities that everything starts with God, and he puts special effort in placing energy and time with his greatest treasure on earth—his family!

Virg is a very curious person by nature and has a well thought out strategy for doing business at a much higher level. He is relentless about pursuing any ventures with purpose and strives for excellence. Christoffels and Company, built from scratch, was recognized as the 'Top Salon' in the nation. Indeed a monumental milestone in business!

Virg is very intentional about doing life and business with excellence. I love his story on the 'how to's' of life and business; not just ordinary—but like Virg says—'*Do Life Big*'!"

Virgil D. DeJongh
Author, Veteran Founder of The DeJongh Financial
Group CEO, DeJongh Publishing and Consulting

"Whether you own a business or are looking for direction in your life, *Do Life Big*, by Virg Christoffels demonstrates the reason why you plan. He gives you tried and true action steps to establish your own plan and lays out a clear path for your business and for you personally. Life is too short to just wing it, '*Do Life Big*'!"

Meredith Dekker
Founder of Meredith Dekker Financial Services LLC,
and Author of The Fabric of a Storyteller

"Working closely with Virg to develop a succession plan, I witnessed his deliberate planning and growth as a husband supporting his wife with cancer. I recommend Virg as a fundamental part to crafting your exit strategy."

Jim Rieffenberger
Leadership Coach

"As a Dale Carnegie trainer for over forty years, I always find it inspiring to see a client use the experiences of the training room to make drastic differences in the business room. Virg Christoffels is a crystal-clear example of being a lifelong learner, taking every opportunity for growth that we had to offer, engaging his staff in the process and then putting ideas into a continuous action plan that helped build and grow his company. Successful business doesn't just happen. Virg Christoffels has always had a vision for success, a plan of action, and a trained team to make it all a reality."

Duane Salonen
Dale Carnegie Trainer

"I never realized how working with a consultant, especially one as genuine and open-minded as Virg, could make such a positive impact on my business. He helped me put together a solid business plan that helped me hire new staff and rapidly grow my business. He does a great job customizing a coaching plan for each individual and making reachable goals not only for the business but for your own personal growth."

April Otis
Final Touches Salon

"Virg is highly respected in the hair replacement industry, so I knew I wanted him to come spend a few days with me and my staff. He helped me revise my business model with concrete goals in place that would give me the time I needed to work *on* my business instead of *in* my business. Virg is also a master stylist, so he was able to work with some of my staff who needed to improve their skill set. He gave 100 percent of his talent and business experience the entire time we spent together. Before his departure, he gave me a summary of everything we discussed and a plan of action to move forward. My business is forever changed in a positive way. Thank you, Virg!"

Tarye Nash
Fused Hair Studio

"The description of a mentor is someone who is experienced and is a trusted advisor, this describes Virg.

Having always admired Virg and his ethical and successful business vision, we jumped at the chance to work directly with him. In this ever evolving industry he helped us look deep and focus on fine tuning our business and really look at it from another point of view. We also applied his theory into our personal lives, with great success!"

Wendy Taylor and Sally Peace
co-owners of Advance Techniques VA

"I had the good pleasure of working with Virg and his daughter Sara. They were executing well on a thoughtful and strategic plan to transition ownership and leadership. Virg is a humble coachable leader who appreciates and considers outside perspectives. He was able to pass this trait on to Sara. As a result, the transition was seamless and the business model he developed is serving the next generation well."

Tony E. Trussel
Business Whyse

DO

SPINNING THE WHEEL OF LIFE TO WIN

LIFE

IN HEALTH, FAMILY, FINANCES, AND FAITH

BIG

VIRG CHRISTOFFELS

THRONE
PUBLISHING GROUP

Cover Design: Mark Henderson
Lead Writer: Marguerite Bonnett
Editor: Liza O'Neal
Publishing Manager: Alle Byeseda

Throne Publishing Group
1601 E 69th St #306
Sioux Falls, SD 57108
ThronePG.com

TABLE OF CONTENTS

PART TWO: YOUR BUSINESS PLAN

PART THREE: YOUR LEGACY PLAN

DEDICATION

To Cheryln, my high school sweetheart, who I grew with and discovered life.

Cheryln and I often attributed the success in our relationship to the fact that we grew up together. Much of our life together was spent in survival mode forcing us to depend on God and each other. Our 46 years of marriage were spent *"Doing Life Big"*. Although we did not know it at the time, God knew our "someday" would come quicker than we thought it would.

Not every part of our life was beautiful, but every part was full! Cheryln was the quiet force encouraging me when needed and often protecting me from myself. She brought balance to our lives, whether it was raising our children or growing our business. When I would spend time worrying, she would spend her time praying with confidence that "all will be well."

After Cheryln's cancer journey ended, the examples she had set motivated me to look at where my life has been, begging the question, "How do I go on from here and bring purpose and value to myself and to others?". I found the answers to that question by reading Cheryln's many prayer journals and the beautiful letters that she left for Sara and Jeremy, Nathan and Holly, our six grandchildren, and for me to read after her death.

Cheryln has provided a path for me to go on, having given me permission to love again. She has provided a way for me to find new purpose and value in my life.

Forever grateful,

Virg
Husband, friend and soulmate

FOREWORD: FROM SARA AND NATHAN

Imagine for a moment; you head to the doctor one day to get a persistent cough checked out. Out of nowhere you are diagnosed with stage 4 lung cancer … that was my mom a few short years ago. If you were watching this story unfold from the outside, you would have seen two of the strongest people grab ahold of their faith and step up to take this head on like you've never seen before. My mom and dad were not going to let this "cancer" define them, or their relationships, or any of the goals they had set for themselves. They were ready to get busy living, and were for sure not going to live like one of them was dying!

Having worked alongside my parents in the family hair replacement business for seventeen years, I learned early on that setting goals is a way of life. You never stop planning; you accomplish one goal after another and then push to conquer the next. We had a major business expansion in the works and implementation upon us during this time. The easy route would have been to back down or to put the expansion on hold. Instead, it was full speed ahead because we had worked hard putting multiple goals in place to continue to grow the business. As I look back on that time, we would not be the business we are today if my dad had chosen to lift his foot off the gas. My mom, of course, was behind all of this 100%—she was always his biggest cheerleader but yet always the calm to his storm.

As I grew up, I have had the privilege of a front row seat, watching and absorbing his habits (even a few of the bad ones). He was constantly reading books, taking classes, and picking the brains of successful people every chance he could get. He was never afraid to admit he didn't know something or to try something that no one had ever tried before. He was constantly trying to find a way to think out of the box. I'll never forget thinking to myself, "when I take over the business, do I need to go into the office on New Year's Eve to set out my goals for the next year?" He always had a general plan for the year, but he made sure goals were very specific. He would tell me that I needed to write down my goals no matter how crazy or simple they might seem. One of the best examples I have is from when I got married and moved away. This really shifted my dad's goal of being able to sell me the business someday. At the time it was crazy to think that I would ever move back to town. But guess what!? Soon after I moved away, I did move back! I found out later that my dad had written a letter expressing that he hoped and prayed that I would move back to town some day. To me, it was crazy to see how his specific goals happened just as he had wished and, as you know, written down.

My dad's goal driven personality took him from a farm doing chores, to a Sioux Falls Taco John's restaurant picking out bad beans one at a time, then entering barber school without ever having had a professional haircut in his life, all the way to owning one of the largest and most successful hair restoration studios in the country. My friends, you don't do that by *not* taking risks and *not* pushing forward hard every day.

Sara Tims
Daughter, Owner and President
of Christoffels Hair Restoration

If you are trying to get the most out of life, then this book is for you. While many business and sales books focus on the latest trick, quick fix, process or magic bullet, this book focuses on the journey. It is a career story that involves hard work, relationships, and success.

On hard work: My sister and I both grew up actively involved in high school sports. Neither of us were ever the star athlete but that didn't mean we didn't think we should be. One night after a basketball game I came home frustrated with my performance and lack of playing time. I vented to my parents about this frustration and my dad responded with one word, "SIAMOA." I guess it was a made up word but it was one he used often. Success Is A Matter Of Attitude, he would say. What I needed to learn is that a person's attitude determines how you approach each day. Positive things happen when you approach life with the right attitude. This is true during those high school sports as well as any career.

On Relationships: Virg is the Type A personality that is ambitious, outgoing, impatient, and likes to stay busy. With that dominant personality, I used to think he was the decision maker in the house, but boy was I wrong! Behind every successful man is a strong woman and that was certainly the case with my mom. While she was more reserved, thoughtful, and planned, I didn't figure out until I was an adult that she was actually calling all the shots. They shared a one of a kind relationship that was an excellent example of how a Christian couple should live. My mom was special. You have to be special to work all day with my dad and still want to have dinner with him at night. Kidding aside, she was special because she was a living example of having that positive attitude. She was always positive regardless of her circumstances. She made my dad better and he couldn't have been that ambitious, outgoing, impatient man without her.

On Success: How many of you write out your goals? It can be a sticky note, a notebook or a napkin but my dad always taught us to write out our goals. In fact, I still have the list of first goals my wife and I wrote out together. It's fun to look back and see how one's perspective on what's important in life has changed. It's also important to look back and be able to see what you've accomplished. To know where you are going, you need to know where you've been. I'm convinced that this simple practice is a life changer. What's the point of making a goal if you don't write it down and create a plan to achieve it?

If you are serious about getting the most out of life then you may already know a thing or two about hard work with the right attitude, building relationships that last forever, and achieving your goals. This book will strengthen your perspective on those things. My hope is that this book and story add value to your life the way my parents and dad have.

Nathan Christoffels
Son, Director—Commercial Execution (West Area)

INTRODUCTION

Thank you for picking up my book. My sincere intention (beyond creating an enjoyable read) is that this book gives you valuable resources that can help you find more time and avoid unnecessary stresses along your journey of building a business while enjoying life.

Whether you are looking to start a business, grow an existing business, or create a succession plan for your business that helps ensure that what you spent a good chunk of your life creating can live on … this book is for you! I want you to win big!

I started out with a high school education, bought a small business, became a lifelong learner, and refined my process at every step. With the help of God, my family, and some amazing coaches and mentors, I managed to build that business into a solid success. And when the time came, my daughter was able to buy the business and continue to grow it, all while keeping peace in the family and putting God first. I guess you could say, I learned a few things that I am excited to share.

If you're serious about building a significant business with balance, profitability, and transferability, this book can serve as a roadmap to get you there. I don't just include stories and how tos, I give you actual downloadable tools you can use that have been proven to help your business succeed.

My Christian faith has always been the first principle that guides and directs my life and my business. My family is a close second to God. I've always believed that if you don't have peace and order in your relationships with God and family, then you will not have peace or order in your business. That's why I begin this book talking about the importance of family and putting God first.

Once you have God and family prioritized in your life, I will introduce you to a very practical, yet life altering way to create a master plan for your business and your life. Every facet of your life is an individual spoke on the wheel that drives your life. Making sure those spokes are balanced will give you a smoother ride and help you to accomplish your dreams. I also share my Life Success Binder and the exact tools that helped me take my business from a one man show to a world class entity.

Finally, I will give you a roadmap for planning your legacy. Whether you want to pass your business on to your heirs or sell it to the highest bidder, there are certain things you need to have in place to ensure your vision and your business lives on.

I hope you enjoy this book. And more importantly, I hope you take away tangible, valuable tools and concepts that can help you succeed beyond your wildest dreams, both in business and in life. And that you have the motivation to start today. Don't wait for someday. *Do Life Big* today!

PART ONE

YOUR PERSONAL PLAN

CHAPTER ONE
GIVE SOMEDAY A DATE

We all have places we want to go, experiences we'd like to have, and things we want to achieve... someday. Haven't we all had those moments in which we allow ourselves to dream of *doing life big*? You know what I'm talking about: those dreams of a lifestyle where you give each day your very best, build towards a legacy that will last for generations, and spend every day grateful for the time God has given. Our big ideas captivate and excite us, but they can seem so far out of reach that oftentimes, our big ideas are relegated to "someday" because someday feels as much as we can handle today.

And then, there are moments in our life when that "someday" that harbors all of our pending hopes and dreams; that "someday" we thought was so far away; suddenly gets a date. This can be an exciting time, or a horrifying time. I've experienced both.

On a crisp, sunny December day in 2011, my wife Cheryln and I were driving from Sioux Falls, South Dakota to Des Moines, Iowa, excited to celebrate Grandparents Day. Our son, Nathan, his wife, Holly, and their three children were anxiously anticipating our arrival at school. Just days before, we had gone to the doctor for some tests. Cheryln had been coughing for about four months, so the doctor took a set of x-rays and said she would call us with the results on Friday. The phone was connected to the car's Bluetooth, ready for the doctor's call.

As we drove, I remember asking Cheryln, "What would you do if the doctor says you had cancer?" I don't remember what she said, just that she remained lighthearted, not wanting to think about that possibility.

> "WHAT WOULD YOU DO IF THE DOCTOR SAYS YOU HAD CANCER?"

Still on the interstate, but nearing the end of our four-and-a-half-hour drive, the phone rang. Cheryln answered and Dr. Klein asked if this was a good time to talk. If not, she could call back on Monday. We did not want to wait till Monday. The doctor proceeded to tell us, "The tests came back and you have a spot on your lung. It's malignant."

We were stunned.

I literally had to pull off the road, and by God's grace, there was an exit right when I needed one. We pulled over to the side of the road and asked the doctor, "What does this mean?"

She explained that there was no question this was cancer and that as soon as we got back, she would help us find the right doctors who would run more tests and figure out what the treatment plan should be. Going from that lighthearted moment to a cancer diagnosis was like getting knocked down to our knees.

We needed to call some people, so we called my closest friend, Virg DeJongh, our pastor, and my oldest brother, who was a minister. He would let our family know. I tried to call my son Nate, but couldn't get a hold of him. So, we called our daughter-in-law Holly and she was able to connect with Nathan. Ironically, Holly's father was also suffering from cancer.

In the parking lot of the school, we prayed for strength. Then we got out of the car, put on our game faces and said, "Okay, let's do this," and walked into the Grandparents Day event. There were a few people there we recognized who greeted us warmly, saying, "How are you guys doing?"

We just said, "Good," and moved on. Somehow, we made it through that whole day without falling apart. Eventually, the phone started ringing and we talked to everybody, getting the message out there.

That night, when we were finally alone, I remember lying in bed. That was when the fear started to descend on us and the tears rolled down our cheeks. But both of us decided we needed to put that away, put on our work boots and declare, "We're going to get through this."

Cheryln was diagnosed on December 3, 2011. She died on February 18, 2018. In our forty-seven years of marriage, we spent countless hours talking about our dreams and making plans. But we didn't have a plan for this. The goals and dreams we create have deadlines. But, so do the things we don't choose.

> "WE'RE GOING TO GET THROUGH THIS."

The doctors appointments began the week after her diagnosis. We never asked, "How long does she have?" We didn't want a date for that someday. But, somewhere along the way, we heard that for the average person with stage four lung cancer, only one percent live three to five years. Cheryln lived for six years, so she liked to call herself a "one percenter." We managed to fit as many somedays into that six years as we could.

Even before the diagnosis, we had a trip planned for our fortieth wedding anniversary. We were taking the kids to the Caymans for a week. Our kids were with us in that first big meeting with all the doctors where they laid out the whole plan. They prescribed thirty rounds of radiation, plus chemo. This was the middle of December and we were scheduled to leave on April 1st. They were a bit lackadaisical about when we should start. We were more concerned about when we would finish so we could take our trip that was already booked. Since time was of the essence, they put the port in on Friday and started treatment on Monday. The goal was to be done by March 19th, giving Cheryln almost two weeks of rest before the trip. She was very beaten up by the treatment, but she wasn't going to miss this trip.

Cheryln had a large tumor about the size of a fist on her left lung and a small spot on her right lung. They treated the large tumor and said they would watch the small one. They couldn't operate on the large tumor because of its location. Plus, it had already metastasized into some lymph nodes. The treatment didn't get rid of the tumor, but it stopped it from growing and even shrunk it a little. By December 2012, the small one started to grow, so we went to the Mayo Clinic where they were able to surgically remove it. Throughout this time, she was on an oral chemo drug.

That first round of treatment got her to December of 2012 when the tumor in the left lung started to grow again. The doctors described her condition as a "gorilla" in her system. The drug acts like a fence, walling off the gorilla. But eventually, the gorilla finds its way around the fence and they have to find a new drug. She was on something until the day she died.

She did have some good times. For almost a year, Cheryln was on one pill that was really effective for her. In the summer of 2013, we were at our condo on Green Lake in Minnesota. I remember seeing an ad on TV for a Rhine River cruise, and I said, "We need to do that." I looked it up on the computer, got on the phone and asked a whole bunch of questions, then booked it that day. I knew that if I didn't approach our goals and dreams with urgency, they wouldn't happen. The trip was for the following summer, which meant we had to put our focus on making it to next summer.

In December of 2013, the tumor on the left lung started to grow again. In January, she started a new drug. One of the side effects of the drug was that it burned her skin. Her face would turn beet red and I remember seeing her in front of the mirror with tweezers peeling off flaking skin. It was very painful. She couldn't smile because it hurt. By summer, the doctor said she needed to take a break, so we stopped it. That allowed us to go to Europe and do that Rhine River cruise and really enjoy it.

When we got back from the trip, she started to get fluid building up in her lungs. They put in a tube and about every five days, we would drain the fluid off. Doing this ourselves kept her out of the hospital and improved our quality of life. Before that, there were many trips to the hospital when she would suddenly have a hard time breathing. In the emergency room, they would give her oxygen and drain the fluid. I could write a book about how to improve customer service in emergency rooms. They have got to be the worst places in the world. You walk in and try to speak through this little window as all these people are sitting there listening to you explain the problem, starting from scratch. So much for medical privacy.

I remember being up at our lake condo when Cheryln was having horrible pain in her abdomen. We got to the emergency room in Willmar,

Minnesota at around one o'clock in the morning and Cheryln said, "I don't think I want to go in there. Let's just get some medication at Walmart." But the second worst place in the world is Walmart in Willmar, Minnesota at one o'clock in the morning. We got some Fleets, but that didn't work. We finally ended up in the emergency room where they found she had a blocked colon, so they took her back to Sioux Falls by ambulance for surgery. It was unrelated to the cancer, but that's one example of how frustrated we had become with emergency rooms.

We took a number of trips throughout this time, including trips to California to see my mother and family living there. We were planning to go out for my mother's 90th birthday party and celebration, but Cheryln had started treatment and we were not able to be there. To our surprise, my family turned my mother's birthday party into a "support Cheryln party" by having T-shirts printed with the words, "We wear pearl for Cheryln." (Pearl is the color used for lung cancer.) Cheryln and I were able to participate by watching on Zoom.

The industry marketing group I belong to has two meetings a year in different locations and she was always there. One aspect of our business is working with people going through medical hair loss, mainly chemo. So, when Cheryln lost her hair, we made a video where she told her story about going through cancer, losing her hair, and what it meant to her to have hair replacement during that time. We wanted to show people that we had empathy for what they were going through, that there is something they could do, and how good it can look. Sara and I were both in the video and it was a big part of our business. We used it as a commercial and we gave everyone in our marketing group permission to use it in their studios around the country. It was very emotional, but it was a positive thing because that's what Cheryln wanted it to be.

For a while, Cheryln kept working. She did all our bookkeeping, HR, and payroll. But after the first year of treatment, we realized she couldn't keep that up.

For six years, we were in and out of the hospital. We were a team. I was blessed to be able to take her to almost every doctor's appointment, except for a couple. I wasn't going to let her go by herself or rely on somebody else to take her.

One of the greatest blessings of having a solid business plan in place was that it allowed me to do that. I was also fortunate that my daughter Sara was a big part of my business and could take on my role. I had a lot of flexibility that I would not have had without a good staff and a good plan in place.

It was a long process. When we first found out, friends suggested we get signed up on CaringBridge, a free website that keeps family and friends connected during health events. Keeping everyone up to date on what's happening can be cumbersome and exhausting. Having one place to post news and receive messages of support is very practical. But we were just not ready for it at that time. It seemed like a death sentence. We were here to go through this treatment and then, it will be gone. So, we're not doing that. We're going into this fight strong because we have life to live.

She went through the treatment and it did beat her up. People kept asking us to start a CaringBridge, almost to the point where it was irritating. I understand now, they all just wanted to know how she was doing, to make communication easier for us, and to know how and what to pray for. But, that was our attitude from December to March 19th. Then, we had to wait three months to see if the treatment was successful.

One morning, we were sitting at home. We have this little nook where we had our coffee in the morning, and in the evening, we would sit and talk. It was our little gathering spot. One morning, she was feeling really terrible and she started to talk in a negative way about her health and the possibility of not surviving.

I looked at her and said, "Cheryln, you're living like you're going to die, you're not living to live." Part of me felt like a bulldog for saying it, but I was trying to be a motivator, trying to give her encouragement. "We've got life to live. You've got things to do and you're not going to win this battle if you're down in the dumps."

She always talked about that later on. I remember her sharing that story with someone and saying, "You know, I've got to start living like I'm going to *live*, not like I'm living to die." She also said, "He only ever had to say that to me once." That was a big milestone.

The whole cancer journey was filled with ups and downs. There was always some little event that would give her a lift. She would go to the doctor and get good news and fly high for a little while. For every PET scan, we'd sit there in front of a big screen waiting for the doctor. He would come in and want to visit, but we just wanted to cut to the chase and see the slides. Sometimes it was good news, sometimes it was bad. It was like betting on a horse race. We used to look at the doctor's face to see if we could predict if it would be good news or bad.

By December of 2012, when the cancer was starting to grow again, Cheryln realized that she needed to be able to communicate with people. That's when Caring-Bridge became a valuable tool for her. It became her ministry. I think she did as much to encourage others as they did to encourage her. Her posts were always positive. Whenever she posted about herself, it was never negative. She was always looking forward to some event that she had to feel good and have the strength for. She would hope that whatever drug she was taking would work so she could go to Europe, or the Caymans, or California.

"YOU KNOW, I'VE GOT TO START LIVING LIKE I'M GOING TO *LIVE*, NOT LIKE I'M LIVING TO DIE."

Cheryln was a journaler and after she died, I read a lot of her journals. Many of them were prayer journals where she had lists of names, from the grandkids, to the kids, to friends that she prayed for. She wrote down bible texts and she found so much encouragement in them.

Towards the end, around November or December of 2017, we found out that the cancer drug she was on was no longer working. That's when it became clear that there was not much more we could do to solve this. That was the moment where we went from living to live, to living with a date. We didn't know the exact date, but we knew it was coming. That was the lowest I ever saw her. In that low moment, she posted something on CaringBridge about really feeling down and not knowing what the next step was going to be. She got so many responses, over fifty, from people who shared Bible texts with her. I still have a copy of that today. It was an encouraging thing for her at that point and it got her out of that slump. At the end of the day, it's important to focus on what actually matters.

Throughout this journey, we were always aware that people were watching. It challenged both of us, but I think it especially challenged Cheryln to put her best foot forward; to smile when she didn't feel like smiling; to go out there and meet the world when she didn't feel like meeting the world. I think it reminded both of us that this is not the time for a pity party. Cheryln's dad always used to say, "Everybody has their cross to bear." We knew our kids were watching us. It was important to leave a good message for them on how to navigate this kind of experience in a positive way.

I BELIEVE CANCER DIDN'T COME BY ACCIDENT. GOD ALLOWED IT TO HAPPEN FOR A REASON. MAYBE A LOT OF REASONS.

I believe cancer didn't come by accident. God allowed it to happen for a reason. Maybe a lot of reasons. This book might be one of them, I don't know. I think part of it was to force me to step away from my business so we could do our someday. If I hadn't, I'd probably still be working every day and have a little different approach to life.

We've had a timeshare in the Caymans for over twenty years and we went there every winter. We got to know people there who became good friends. Because we saw the same people every year, they followed Cheryln's journey. On the day of her funeral, they watched it online. Then, about twenty of them gathered up flowers, walked down to the ocean and floated the flowers out onto the water. That was a special time because these people were from all different faiths, and at different places in their spiritual journey. Just to know that people cared that much really meant a lot. It was also an affirmation that Cheryln touched and encouraged a lot of people.

The main theme here is, life didn't stop. If anything, it got kicked into a higher gear. We did more things, more deliberately. Whenever we were on a trip, we were always planning the next one. When people have a date, it changes them. They begin to live intentionally and deliberately. We could almost chuckle at people who were working non-stop because they figured, "We'll do that someday." We all have a date on us, we just don't know when that will come. But in Cheryln's case, we knew she had cancer and we knew she wasn't going to survive it. With that, it becomes pretty easy to be intentional and deliberate.

We hardly ever talked about her dying and that too was intentional. When we decided to live to live, not live to die, that set the stage for not talking about dying. Of course, she wrote her funeral plans and her obituary. We bought a head stone and burial plots. That was very deliberate. We even took people out there before she died to show them the headstone. It was kind of like buying a new car. I think she was afraid I would get a pink stone or something she would never choose. So, she got to pick out what she wanted.

Right before we went to the Caymans for the last time, she was having a really hard time breathing. We went to the hospital and had them drain her lungs. We were worried about that happening in the Caymans, so they put the tube back in. I knew how to drain it, but not a lot came out when we were on that trip. Even then, we never talked about dying. We never talked about how this was probably our last trip to the Caymans. When we flew back into Chicago, she said, "I need a wheelchair to get to the other gate." We got a wheelchair and stopped at the bar for a glass of wine. We took a picture there and when I looked at it later, I thought, oh man, she looks so frail. That's when the lights started coming on for me.

When we got home Saturday night, she asked me to drain the fluid, but nothing came out. She was having a hard time breathing. Monday, we called the doctor and on Thursday, we went in. He told us we could come back tomorrow to get a chest x-ray, or he could admit us to the hospital and we could get it that day. Without hesitating, we decided on the hospital.

The doctor told us to be prepared to answer the end of life questions like, "Do you want extra measures to sustain life?" We had never had that conversation before.

She was admitted on a Thursday. I was there all day, then went home that night. I was back on Friday, spent the day, and was headed home Friday night at about nine o'clock when the nurse called and said "We've moved her down to the pulmonary unit. You should come back." I asked if I should be prepared to stay the night and he said yes. So, I gathered up some clothes and headed back. She had been put on a BiPAP machine for oxygen. It was hard to communicate with her because I couldn't hear her under that mask. Sara was there with me, but my son and his family were living in New Jersey. The doctor said we should call him. He got a ticket and was to arrive home at 11:30pm on Saturday. That night, I was trying to sleep in a chair next to the hospital bed when a nurse came in. She asked Cheryln how she was doing and I'll ever forget what she said. She took that oxygen mask off and said, "My son is coming home tomorrow at 11:30. After that, I'm done." Sitting there in the dark, I didn't say anything, but that was news to me.

The next morning, Sara was back and we were asking the doctor what was going to happen here. Did we need to go to hospice? The doctor was evasive long enough for us to get the message that we wouldn't need to worry about hospice.

On Sunday, she really couldn't talk, so there wasn't a lot of conversation. Nathan had arrived on Saturday at 11:30 p.m. and Holly and the grandkids were to arrive at 11:30 Sunday night. We were letting her rest so she would have the energy to visit with them when they arrived. A few family members came by to see her and our pastor stopped in a number of times on Saturday and Sunday. About three in the afternoon, Cheryln asked to see me. She pulled her mask off and said, "I'm ready to go." I hugged her and told her they would start the morphine and she said, "I know." I said, "We won't be able to talk anymore." She said, "I'm ready to go" and gave me a thumbs up.

"WE WON'T BE ABLE TO TALK ANYMORE." SHE SAID, "I'M READY TO GO" AND GAVE ME A THUMBS UP.

I sat with her for a while after they started the morphine. Then I asked her, "What are you seeing? Are you seeing heaven?" She said, "I'm seeing flowers." But the mask garbled her words and I thought she said something about a black ceiling. I said, "A black ceiling?" She pulled that mask off and said, "No dummy, I'm going to heaven, not hell." And those were the last words she said.

Our relationship was so close, we didn't have to talk about it. She knew what I was going to say before I said it. It was almost as if we could read each other's minds. There was nothing left unsaid. The only thing left was to let the doctor know her heart had stopped. The kids were there and we just prayed for a while.

After that, to Cheryln's credit, everything was planned. It was just like in our business. She had it all written out: who the pallbearers would be, what songs were to be sung, what Bible passages were going to be read, how the grandkids would participate in the service.

We had the burial first, then the funeral service in the church, which was a celebration of life. We had a big picture of her dressed as classy as she could be. It wasn't a sad time. It was emotional. And I think there was a sense of relief for me and for our family that this trial was over.

I chose to start this book with Cherlyn's and my story to impress upon my readers how important it is to start *Doing Life Big* right now. There will always be reasons to wait, but time is a gift that should never be taken for granted. No matter what reasons you might have to wait. I assure you there are more reasons not to wait. Whether it's a business goal, a goal to start a family, or to go on a tropical vacation… give your goals a date. You can start working towards and achieving goals today even in the smallest ways. Live every day intentionally and deliberately. Then give it your heart.

CHAPTER TWO

YOUR MOST IMPORTANT PARTNERS

Being raised in a Christian home, going to a Christian day school, and having a family that always went to church, it was instilled in me early that God was really important. After God, your most important relationship in life is your spouse. If these two relationships are not optimal, nothing else will be.

I didn't have a full appreciation of my partnership with God during the first years of my marriage to Cheryln. We were still young and thought we were in control of our own game plan.

When I think back to when we were first married, we were just starting out in life and a little excited about all the beautiful things in the world. All the stuff. We did God, but not in the same context that we would think about God today. God was something we did when we were kids growing up. My family had a dairy farm and every morning, we would have breakfast as a family before school. We sat around the table and had devotions and read the Bible. The bus could be at the end of the driveway, but we didn't go out until we had prayed and read the Bible.

Cheryln also grew up in a Christian home, attended a Christian school, and went to the same denomination church. We started first grade together, and our lives just meshed from about the age of seven years old. We got engaged when we were seniors in high school. Her birthday was in April and I sold everything I had for $180 and bought her a diamond ring. Who does that in high school?

> OUR MARRIAGE BECAME BASED ON PUTTING GOD FIRST AND WE TRIED TO IMPRESS THAT ON OUR KIDS.

Once we were on our own and started making decisions for ourselves, we wanted to do all these new things we had never tried before. But, after we started our family, we began to have a different appreciation for the way we lived our life. So, we decided to double down on our relationship with God. Basically, we started to mature. As my relationship with God grew, it allowed me to make better decisions. We prayed about things and contemplated them from a spiritual standpoint, rather than just from an Earthly perspective.

PUT GOD FIRST

Our marriage became based on putting God first and we tried to impress that on our kids by sending them to a Christian school where our values would be reinforced. We went to church on Sunday and, in essence, we had a fairly normal home. Was it perfect? No. But, by the grace of God, we avoided having any big wrecks.

At the same time, we were in the first years of growing our business. Cheryln was a homemaker and working to take care of the kids while I worked on the business. Once the kids were in school, she got more involved in the business. We were both also involved in leadership opportunities that gave us a chance to demonstrate and express our faith. It was obvious to everyone that God was a big deal in our lives. Especially when we got to the cancer journey. That journey was not easy, but it was easier because God was there. I have been to funerals, and visitations. I have met with people who have lost a loved one, but didn't have God in their life.

It seems to me that those are the people who cry the hardest and scream the loudest. And maybe they have reason to. I think we were able to go through this and have a lot of sadness, but also a sense of peace and confidence that God will heal us and walk us through the lessons we need to learn. I believe that was because we tried to put God first in our life.

Cheryln and I fed off each other. When she began to think about dying, I was able to encourage her. Throughout our life together, I spent a lot of time in worry and fear. Whether it was a financial crisis or something else, she was always the one who talked me off the ledge. I know how many prayers were said by her for me. She was always right there with me and God was number one.

> WHEN YOU HAVE A STRONG FAITH IN GOD AND YOU LIVE THAT EVERY DAY, IT GIVES YOUR LIFE A WHOLE DIFFERENT PURPOSE AND MEANING.

When you have a strong faith in God and you live that every day, it gives your life a whole different purpose and meaning. It allows you to see the big picture. Even if there's something fearful today, I know that it is going to go away. It's not always that God will simply take it away, but that He gives it to me for a reason. Sometimes I need to see something. Sometimes I need to slow down, be aware, or appreciate something. But I know, that problem is going to go away. Many times, I have prayed saying, "I don't know how this is all going to work out, but I'm just going to put it into your hands." And one day, I look back and think, that worked out. Sometimes, I even remember to say, "Thanks."

I try to live life knowing God is over everything. That doesn't mean we lived a perfect life, but putting God first was our goal, in our marriage, in the way we treated each other, the way we treated our kids, the way we wanted our kids to treat us, and how we operated in business. The hair restoration marketing group I belonged to is called Transitions. A lot of the members are at different places in their faith and spiritual walk. I was occasionally asked to give presentations at our bi-annual meetings, so they all knew me and it was a great opportunity to demonstrate my faith; to be an example to people through our relationship.

I remember way back when I first started doing hair replacement, I was at a training event in Florida. At lunch, I was sitting with a guy from New York. I heard so many shocking conversations there; stories people told about the way they were living their life. It was like poison. I said to this guy, "I can't be a part of that. I don't know if I can be a Christian and be in this business." Thankfully, he was a Christian and he said to me, "You can. And we need people like us here to let people know that God can be evidence and prevail in every circumstance." And, of course, God provided many opportunities for me to express my faith and be an example.

God also plays a huge role in our family. There are plenty of books on parenting, but the best one to read is the Bible. It's pretty black and white. For example, our kids knew that if they ever disrespected their mother, there would be consequences. And they knew it was a spiritual thing. We were fortunate that we were able to raise our kids through high school and college without anyone getting into trouble with drugs, drinking, or serious behavior issues. I totally give God credit for guiding us through that. Perhaps it was just our routine, because that's how we were raised. If so, it's a pretty good routine. It was tested and proven by our parents, and their parents. The Bible talks a lot about how things flow from one generation to the next. It's such a joy to witness how putting God first gets validated when I see my kids demonstrating this way of life to their kids.

MAKE GOD AND YOUR SPOUSE PRIORITIES

My most intentional relationships are with God and my spouse. The respect that I had for Cheryln and the respect that she had for me came from what we learned in the Bible, from going to church, and from other Christian friends. I had to learn some of those things the hard way. I'm sure I asked for a lot of forgiveness.

I learned a lot about being a husband, a father, and now a grandfather from Cheryln's dad. He was the eighty-year-old grandpa who would sit on the floor with the grandkids and play with them. He had the ultimate respect for his wife. He waited on her hand and foot. He got that from God. It came down through the generations, like we learned in the Bible.

MY MARRIAGE WITH CHERYLN WAS BASED ON GOD BEING THE CENTER OF OUR RELATIONSHIP.

My marriage with Cheryln was based on God being the center of our relationship. That was demonstrated through the whole cancer journey. Prayer was the first place we turned when we found out Cheryln had cancer. In fact, we put God first in all our challenging times.

The first time Cheryln got pregnant, she had a miscarriage. At about the five month appointment, the doctor could not find a heartbeat anymore. At that time, they didn't take the baby, so she had to carry it for another two months before he was finally delivered. That was very hard on her. At that point in our lives, I wasn't as sensitive as I should have been. We all have times of failure and breakdown. Those moments are for God to get our attention. When He has you in a corner and you've got no place else to go, that's when you remember to go to your knees and to go to scripture.

UNITY

It was important for Cheryln and I to be on the same page; to be united and in agreement. We were a team. We had to be for our marriage to work and not be pulled apart by me making a decision to do something with the business and her not being on board. That would never work. We needed to be pulling in the same direction. Our goals had to be the same in every aspect of our life, whether it was about how we wanted to raise our kids, where we wanted them to go to school, or how we wanted the business to function. We had to be united. And we especially had to be united in front of our kids.

If our kids ever saw a division, it wouldn't have worked. It would tear the family apart. If kids see a crack in their parents' relationship, they're going to go for the crack. If they're able to put a wedge between parents, it opens the door for them to do whatever they want. There's nothing that will ruin parenting or kids faster than a breakdown between mom and dad.

COMMUNICATION

Cheryln and I talked about everything. Our drive up to the lake took three hours and in summer, we did that almost every weekend. We talked the whole way. That was our planning time. That was our dreaming time. We were always dreaming about what we would do next and how it was going to work. Cheryln was always the first person I went to with my ideas. She would listen, and in her soft-spoken way, I got affirmation about whether I should or shouldn't do something. She often joked that I made her nervous with my ideas. She used to say, "If you say it, it's probably going to happen."

> OUR GOALS HAD TO BE THE SAME IN EVERY ASPECT OF OUR LIFE, WHETHER IT WAS ABOUT HOW WE WANTED TO RAISE OUR KIDS, WHERE WE WANTED THEM TO GO TO SCHOOL, OR HOW WE WANTED THE BUSINESS TO FUNCTION. WE HAD TO BE UNITED.

We could never understand couples who openly shared how out of agreement they were. If Cheryln and I ever disagreed, we never had that conversation in front of our kids, or anyone else. If you have kids, you need to have a conversation. How do you want to raise your kids? What message do you want to send your kids? Will you just allow them to do whatever they want? I know people mean well, but letting kids do what they think they want forces them to make decisions on their own, when sometimes, they are too young to be making that kind of decision on their own.

We had friends with a ten-year-old at our kid's Christian school. One day they told us, "Well, he decided he wanted to go to public school this year." There is no ten-year-old who is mature enough to decide what school to go to. We told our kids, this is the school the money is going to and that's where you're going. If husband and wife are not on the same page, you can't do that. It's the same with choosing friends, choosing a church, or buying a car. If you're not on the same page, you're setting yourselves up for "I told you so" and a lot of stress, anxiety, uncertainty, and no clarity. It's so important for kids to see a unified front from a mom and dad. If that's not present, the kids suffer, but the mom and dad suffer more. Marriage is a team effort.

ALIGNMENT

Our conversations transformed the day we learned about goal setting. Back in the 1980s, we attended a Zig Ziglar event that changed our lives. Goals became very important to us. God was always first, so our spiritual goals came first, then our relationship goals, family goals, business goals, and recreational goals, in that order. Thankfully, we were always on the same page.

EVERY BIG DECISION IN OUR LIVES WAS A STORY OF US BEING UNITED.

Every big decision in our lives was a story of us being united. Whether it was when I started my own business, or when we changed from cutting hair to doing full time hair replacement, that was a long process that took years of writing down goals, planning, and eventually burning all boats to the past. It was a big deal to let go of our existing livelihood for a new way of doing business and it required Cheryln's affirmation. When we built a building for our business, then built a second building, we got down on our knees and prayed for guidance. Together. And when Cheryln got cancer, we made a unified commitment of, "We can do this."

GOAL SETTING

One of the best ways I know to get people on the same page is to have a common goal. That can be in your business, your relationship, or your family. It's also one of the best ways to *Do Life Big*. If you know you're not on the same page, you have to find a common goal. For Cheryln and I, our first common goal was that whatever we did, it had to honor God, be acceptable to God, and God had to be at the center of all our decisions. If it was right by God, then we could sift through all the other layers.

> WHEN OUR SPIRITUAL LIFE WAS IN ALIGNMENT WITH A GOAL, THEN OUR MARRIAGE COULD COME TOGETHER TOWARDS THAT GOAL. WHEN OUR MARRIAGE WAS IN ALIGNMENT, THEN OUR FAMILY COULD COME TOGETHER. AND WHEN OUR FAMILY WAS IN ALIGNMENT, THEN OUR BUSINESS COULD DEVELOP AND PROSPER.

When our spiritual life was in alignment with a goal, then our marriage could come together towards that goal. When our marriage was in alignment, then our family could come together. And when our family was in alignment, then our business could develop and prosper. If any of the things above the business level is broken, then the business will suffer because you have a distraction going on upstream. When the business comes together, you've got it all. It's a beautiful circle.

When your business is humming along, from that comes financial rewards. These financial rewards allow you to be a good steward. You can do things with your family, take vacations, go on trips, grow your business, and help others. All of those things help your family, they help your kids, and they help your spiritual life. If your business is doing well, you may have time to do some leadership in your church or be a mentor. So, let's break this down into steps.

REVISIT YOUR VISION

Step one is to revisit your vision, or if you don't have one, create one. What do you want your life to look like? Paint that picture. It's like taking a trip. Identify where you want to go. Then, figure out what has to happen to get there. First of all, you have to be on the same page. It all starts with God. Once you're on the same page with God, then get clear on your vision for your relationship, family, and business. Get a notebook and write down all your ideas. Discuss them until you are very clear and in alignment with what you both want.

WRITE YOUR GOALS DOWN

This is crucial. Until you write it down, it's not a goal. It's just a thought. Start with your spiritual goals. For example, I am going to read through the Bible this year. I will do devotions every day. I am going to pray with my kids. Whatever you put in that column is feeding your top goal: Spiritual.

Then go to your relationship with your spouse. What do you need to do in this area this year? Perhaps you need to schedule one date night per month. Maybe you want to send them flowers once a month or to write them a note once a week that says, "What I love about you is…" What do you want to be, do, and have in your relationship? Write it all down. Continue with each area until you have all the goals that, if you do them, will make your vision a reality.

REVIEW MONTHLY

Once you've filled out each area with your goals for the year, you need to review them at least once a month. Ask yourself specific questions. How am I doing with my goal to read through the Bible this year? How did our date night go? Did I pray with my kids? This requires you to be deliberate and intentional. You can write down all those goals and it looks really good. But if you're not deliberate and intentional about checking

BUT IF YOU'RE NOT DELIBERATE AND INTENTIONAL ABOUT CHECKING ON YOUR PROGRESS, THE WHOLE THING BECOMES MEANINGLESS.

on your progress, the whole thing becomes meaningless. It's like taking a trip from the West Coast to the East Coast. You need to check your progress along the way, make sure you're on the right road, and at the right point by the right time to get to your destination.

Now that you and your spouse are united, aligned with God, and communicating your vision, let's delve a little deeper into goal setting and living a deliberate and intentional life.

CHAPTER THREE
LIVING A DELIBERATE LIFE

Living intentionally begins with having an idea of the direction you want to go. The danger of living your life without direction is that you end up in survival mode reacting to whatever comes your way. I know people who don't have goals or dreams and just live day to day. They fly by the seat of their pants doing whatever feels good at the moment. Without a goal, you're not working towards anything. Zig Ziglar used to say, "You're just a wandering generality." If you have no goals, you have no blueprint, no plan for where your life is going.

GOAL SETTING

A goal is the declaration of a place you want to get to. Goals add value to your life. They also give you peace of mind knowing that all you have to do is follow the plan. It doesn't mean you can't change it, but you have a plan. For me, there's nothing worse than not knowing what I'm going to do tomorrow and having nothing to say about it. When I have goals, I'm more purposeful. Everything I do builds towards something. I'm not just spending my energy, I'm investing my energy. Goals are motivating. They challenge you to be a better person. And a happy side effect is that you become a more fulfilled person. I have been using what I call my Life Success Binder for over forty years and it has been my key tool for creating both the business and the life of my dreams. I want to share this extraordinary system with you because I know it can transform your business, and your life as well.

A GOAL IS THE DECLARATION OF A PLACE YOU WANT TO GET TO. GOALS ADD VALUE TO YOUR LIFE. THEY ALSO GIVE YOU PEACE OF MIND KNOWING THAT ALL YOU HAVE TO DO IS FOLLOW THE PLAN.

When I started writing goals, it changed everything. It all started the day Cheryln and I attended that half-day Zig Ziglar seminar. We drank the Kool-Aid and bought all the books and tapes. I listened to those tapes every day driving to and from work. I wore out one set and bought another. One day, we had gone to a barber meeting in southwest Minnesota where we heard a speaker talk about the power of setting goals. That night, driving home in the dark, we started to talk about all the things we wanted to do. But, we had no paper. Cheryln looked around and grabbed a paper sack from the backseat, turned on the dome light, and started writing down all the things we wanted to accomplish and everything we needed to do to get there. A lot of these were business goals, one of which was, we wanted to stop cutting hair and become a full-time hair replacement studio. That was the first time we wrote that down. And we kept writing it down for eight years before we finally achieved it.

An interesting thing happens when you write down a goal. It focuses your thoughts and efforts, both consciously and subconsciously, towards your goal. We kept dreaming and asking, what if? I knew I needed to start selling more hair. So, I reached out to other people who did full time hair replacement to learn how they did it and I used that information to start selling more hair. Hair pieces come in boxes, which I began to collect and put on the shelf near where I was cutting hair. Customers would look over, see all these boxes, which they didn't know were empty, and say, "You've got a lot of hair you're selling." We gave people the perception that, if they ever needed it, I was the hair replacement guy. We started doing some advertising and, pretty soon, we became known as the place to go for hair replacement.

After eight years of working toward our goal, the day finally came when we decided to pull the trigger and fully commit to our vision. We had 200 regular customers coming to us for haircuts. We sent them all a letter saying we are no longer doing that. We are now a full-time hair replacement studio. Giving up that income stream was an act of faith and commitment, because once those letters hit the mailbox, there was no going back. I remember getting a few calls from friends saying, "I've never been fired by my barber before." I gave all my customers to Steve Klooster, a friend of mine who owned a professional hair salon. I could have sold the business, but I didn't even think about that at the time. I was more interested in making sure they were taken care of and I was focused on my new business model of full time hair replacement.

I had one employee who had been cutting hair for us for twelve years. When I told her we were not going to be doing that anymore, she responded by letting me know that she wanted to continue to work in a barber shop. So, I asked her, "Do you want to leave?" She left. She was a good employee, but that was just another part of burning the boats.

NEW HOUSE GOALS

In 1976, we bought our first house on East 26th Street. In 1979, our daughter Sara was three years old and we wanted to get off that busy street. So, we bought a house in the country on a gravel road in the Pine Hill Subdivision. A few years later, we decided to put in a pool. It was one of my many wild ideas, but it fit with my goal of creating a close, happy family. I talked to the pool people in the fall and they said, "If you pay a one third deposit, we can install it now, have you pay one third during the winter, and one third in the spring when we get it up and running. We looked at that hole in the backyard all winter long thinking, "What are we doing?" But it was a great place to raise two kids—and we had everyone else's kids there, too. It made the place look nice and we really had fun out there.

When Sara was out of high school, we set a goal to buy a different house. We looked at one house on Prairie Green Golf Course that was listed at $140,000 and decided we couldn't afford that, so we spent about $25,000 remodeling our house. We put in a new kitchen and some new windows. Then in 1994, we were driving down a black top street in a new subdivision and saw a lot for sale. We bought that in the fall of 1994 and started building a house the following May. So, after not being able to afford the $140,000 house, we ended up building a $230,000 house. Our desire was to get off that gravel road, which by the way is still gravel today.

That may sound like we were living by the seat of our pants, but Cheryln and I were on the same page of wanting to live in a nice house. That was a goal we both envisioned. We were dreamers. We didn't wrap our goal around how many dollars we needed to do it. We wanted a great place to raise our family. And we wanted a good quality of life. That was our goal.

YOUR MASTER PLAN

Goals are not about knowing exactly where you are going to be every minute. Our goals concerned God, relationship with spouse, family, and business. While it may look like we were being very spontaneous, buying land, putting in a pool, moving to a new house, we were operating within the larger goals for our life. This is where being in alignment with God and with each other comes in. When you are trusting God, writing down your dreams and goals, and taking action towards them, He puts opportunities on your path.

Some people are afraid to write down goals because they don't know where to start. I didn't write down a goal for a pool, or for buying that lot. But they were still a part of our Master Plan. You need to be able to

> WHEN YOU ARE TRUSTING GOD, WRITING DOWN YOUR DREAMS AND GOALS, AND TAKING ACTION TOWARDS THEM, HE PUTS OPPORTUNITIES ON YOUR PATH.

respond to life on a day to day basis, and still fit your actions into that Master Plan. When you are in alignment with God, each other, and your goals, you can take advantage of opportunities. We did a lot of great things that we didn't have written down. But those dreams fit into the larger goals we had set for our life.

Your goals empower you to work through challenges, as well. We did not have a goal for Cheryln to get cancer. But we did have a Master Plan. Our business plan allowed us to work through that enormous challenge.

THE GOAL SETTING PROCESS

Goals are personal. I have a particular framework for creating goals that works for me and my priorities in life. You may have slightly different priorities depending on what is important to you or specific areas you want to focus on.

What is most important to you? You could list spiritual goals, then family goals. Or maybe you want to have separate goals for your relationship with your spouse. If health is a major issue, you may want to move that up the list temporarily. Ask yourself, how do I want to develop my life? How can I be a better person? How can I function more effectively in business? Think of goal categories as all the major components that you need to keep your life running smoothly.

CATEGORIZE YOUR GOALS

Let's start by creating your list of goal categories. What things are most important to you? Here's the list I use, in order of importance for me. Feel free to copy it or tweak it so that it's personal to you.

1. *Spiritual*
2. *Spouse*
3. *Family*
4. *Business*

5. *Health*
6. *Recreation*

Alongside my personal goals, I have my business goals. Those are broken down into:

- *Marketing*
- *Operations*
- *Financial*
- *Special projects*
- *Leads*
- *Consultations*
- *Sales*
- *Customer Service*

> CREATING GOALS CHALLENGES ME TO THINK ABOUT WHERE MY LIFE IS GOING.

There is no magic number of categories. I usually have written goals in at least five or six categories. You may find that a lot of your other goals are sub-categories.

I personally do this at the start of every year. It feels like a lot, until suddenly, a couple of months later, you're looking at your goals and you realize, oh, I can check that off the list. Or, I'm on schedule for that. You accomplish more when you have goals. I am surprised all the time by how much I get done. I am much more effective with goals. And, it takes away a lot of the fear, uncertainty, and wonder about where my life is going.

Creating goals challenges me to think about where my life is going. You may find yourself ratcheting up your goals. If you read eight books last year, maybe you can read twelve books this year. They also help you prioritize your time and plan your week. If there's something really important you need to get done, you may decide to forego that TV time. You can also make a list of the top six things you need to do this week to accomplish or be on track with your goals. As you check more and more things off your list, that sense of accomplishment builds your self worth. That's how you bring value to yourself and live with purpose.

MAKE YOUR GOALS SMART

If you've spent any time around personal growth leaders, you've probably heard of SMART Goals. The term was coined by George Doran in 1981 and has been used by most every consultant, coach, and motivational speaker since, mainly because it works. It's very hard to improve what you don't measure. There are people I've mentored who have never set goals before and I always encourage them to study and implement this formula. Even for experienced goal setters, I don't think we can hear this enough.

When you write out your goals in each category, make sure those goals follow the SMART formula by making them:

The more specific you can be, the more obvious what you have to do to achieve them becomes. Make your goals measurable. If you want to lose weight, how much and by when? If you want to make more money, how much and by when? It's also a good idea to set achievable goals. One of the best ways to do this is to chunk your goals down into realistic pieces or steps. If I want to lose twelve pounds, I can make my goal to lose two pounds a month for the next six months. Financially, you may want to donate a certain dollar amount this year. How much extra do you need to earn a month, or where are you spending money that can be prioritized for giving to make that happen?

> THE MORE SPECIFIC YOU CAN BE, THE MORE OBVIOUS WHAT YOU HAVE TO DO TO ACHIEVE THEM BECOMES. MAKE YOUR GOALS MEASURABLE.

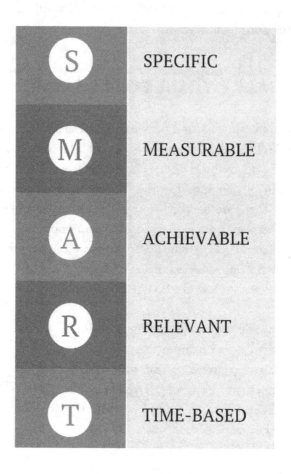

Make your goals specific to whatever is going on in your life at the time. Some of my goals have included journaling four times a week, mentoring or coaching others, speaking at a conference, and reading twelve books in a year. Some people read a book a week, but for me, twelve books a year was a big step. In my personal life, I thought about how I could nurture my family and what things I could do to build a close, healthy, happy family. We decided to build a pool, but you could take your family on a trip or commit to going out on the bike trails together. All these things are measurable. This process is like doing a personal assessment of where you are and where you want to be. When you figure that out, you can then create a set of goals to take you from point A to point B.

REVENUE	
SALES SUPPORT	
MARKETING	
ADMINISTRATIVE	
PROJECTS	
THE "WHY" This is the purpose or reason you are willing to sacrifice your efforts to achieve these outcomes.	
TOP 3 PRIORITIES	

WWW.DOLIFEBIGBOOK.COM/GOALS

There have been times when I had really big, wild goals with no idea how I was going to achieve them. They were more like dreams of something I would like to do *someday.* Those don't really become goals until that thing becomes important. But they are definitely fun to have in the back of your mind.

REVIEW GOALS REGULARLY

Check in on how you're doing with your goals monthly at a minimum. Weekly is better. When I was working in my business, I kept all my goals in my Life Success Binder on my desk. One of the first things I did every Monday morning was look through that binder. My goals would tell me what I had to do that week, and then, I would decide what was most important to work on first. And more importantly, I got to assess how I did the previous week.

When I looked at all the different areas, I might say to myself, "I'm good with my physical goals, my family goals, and my relationship with my wife, but I'm not doing much with my spiritual goals." So, that becomes my reminder to make sure I'm doing devotions four times a week, or getting involved in a Bible study. If my goal was to read through the Bible this year, how much do I need to do every day? For a number of years, my brother LeRoy would put together a plan for me to read through the Bible in one year. You can also type into a search engine, "Read through the Bible in a year" and find a plan for doing that. Your weekly review helps you stay on track, or get back on track.

> WHATEVER YOU DO, MAKE SURE YOU SET ASIDE A SPECIFIC TIME EACH WEEK TO GO OVER YOUR GOALS.

I always made sure to include my family in my goals. An example of family goals might be to get home from work at a specific time, creating a good work life balance. Know what time your kids get home. Maybe make an effort to have dinner together every night or create family time in a different way. Maybe that means on Saturday, I will spend half the day doing something with my kids, without worrying about cleaning the garage or doing yard work.

Whatever you do, make sure you set aside a specific time each week to go over your goals. It could be Monday morning at work, or an evening at home with your spouse. Make reviewing your goals, one of your goals. Every week, look at your goals and think about where you've been and where you are going. Look for new and different opportunities to meet your goals. It's actually very satisfying to create a plan and execute it.

Once you have clear goals, it's time to get your wheel spinning.

CHAPTER FOUR

YOUR PERSONAL
SUCCESS WHEEL

Your Personal Success Wheel is a visual way of looking at your goals. It instantly shows you which areas you need to work on. To create your wheel, use the one in the book, or simply draw a circle on a blank piece of paper. Then, divide the circle into as many sections as you have goal categories. The spokes are your goal categories. For my wheel, I have six categories, so I divided my circle into six pie shaped pieces. Inside the circle, there are five concentric circles starting in the center and moving outward. Each circle represents a value, with number one nearest the center, getting higher as you move toward the outer edge, which is number five.

Label each pie piece section with your most important life categories. Mine are labelled Faith, Spouse, Family, Business, Health, and Recreation.

— LIFE SUCCESS WHEEL ——————— EXAMPLE —
Label important life categories

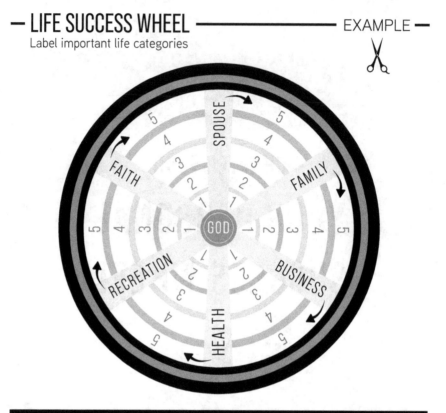

WWW.DOLIFEBIGBOOK.COM/LIFE_SUCCESS_WHEEL

Next, score each one of these categories, from one to five, according to how effectively you think you are meeting your goals in each area. Mark that pie section on the circle that corresponds to your self assessment score.

For example, in Spiritual, let's say you've been going to church on Sundays, but you haven't been meeting your goal to read the Bible or join a Bible study, you might give yourself a three. Highlight the third circle in that section. In family, if you've been spending a lot of extra time with the kids, you might give yourself a four or five. Highlight the corresponding circle in that section. For Spouse, let's say you've been fighting lately, you might give yourself a two. Highlight the second circle in that section. For business, let's say you're doing ok, but you'd like to do much better. Maybe you give yourself a three. So, you highlight the third circle in that section. Continue this process until you have the corresponding circle highlighted in each goal category according to your self assessment.

Now, connect all those circle pieces to see what your wheel looks like. Is your wheel smooth and balanced? Would your wheel roll down the road into your future smoothly? Or, would it be a very bumpy ride?

TRACKING YOUR PROGRESS

Your Personal Success Wheel clearly identifies areas where you are succeeding, as well as problem areas. When you know which goal categories you need to focus extra effort on, you can create a more well-rounded life experience.

Your Personal Success Wheel is an extension of the goal setting process. It helps you be deliberate because you can see exactly where your weak spots are. It makes me accountable to achieve what I set out to achieve.

WOULD YOUR WHEEL ROLL DOWN THE ROAD INTO YOUR FUTURE SMOOTHLY?

If you look at your goals once a week, you can look at your wheel once a month. That's your assessment time. Once a month, you measure how you are doing in each of your goal categories. Then, draw the wheel, print it out, and put it in your Life Success Binder. That way, you can see where you're going month to month. You can instantly see in which areas you've made some headway and which areas are in need of a little attention.

I put God at the center of the circle because, for me, the only reason we do all these things is to glorify God. To be the person I need to be in business, in health, and with my family, I need to have God at the center of it all.

USE REAL DATA

One of the most important aspects of any tracking device is the quality of the information you're using to create the data points. This should not be an emotional exercise. It's not about how good or bad you feel about something. You want to actually look at the goal you set for yourself and take an honest, analytical assessment of where you are with meeting that goal. If your fitness goal is to do sixty pushups by a certain date, how many can you actually do today and are you on track to get to your goal? Score yourself on real data. How many books have you read this month? How much time have you spent with your kids? Are you home for dinner each night or are you working late? Whatever you are measuring, use real input.

> I PUT GOD AT THE CENTER OF THE CIRCLE BECAUSE, FOR ME, THE ONLY REASON WE DO ALL THESE THINGS IS TO GLORIFY GOD.

That input comes from your goals. What makes my Personal Success Wheel different from others' is that it includes your goals around the wheel, so you can accurately assess and track them.

For each category, there is a Goals box where you list your primary goals. Let's say you have six goals for Family. Write those six goals into the Family box. That might look like: Be home for dinner at least five nights a week, take the kids on the bike trails on Saturdays, attend at least one sports event a week, pray with my kids every morning, or whatever is important to your family. Now, you can look at your list and do a real assessment.

When you read through those goals, if you've only achieved three out of six, then draw your line on the circle at 50% progress. Now, this becomes less of an emotional exercise, and more of a real life, honest assessment of where you are with what you said you want. With real data, you can make good decisions about what you need to do next week and next month. We've talked about making your goals measurable. This tool makes them easily and visibly measurable. It becomes your monthly goals scorecard.

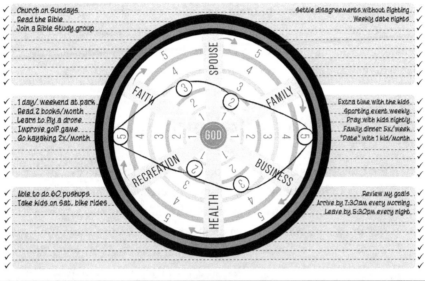

Score each one of these categories, from one to five according to
how effectively you think you are meeting your goals in each area.

✓ Church on Sundays   Settle disagreements without fighting ✓
✓ Read the Bible   Weekly date nights ✓
✓ Join a Bible Study group   ✓

✓ 1 day/ weekend at park   Extra time with the kids ✓
✓ Read 2 books/month   Sporting event weekly ✓
✓ Learn to fly a drone   Pray with kids nightly ✓
✓ Improve golf game   Family dinner 5x/week ✓
✓ Go kayaking 2x/month   "Date" with 1 kid/month ✓

✓ Able to do 60 pushups   Review my goals ✓
✓ Take kids on Sat. bike rides   Arrive by 7:30am every morning ✓
                                                           Leave by 5:30pm every night ✓

WWW.DOLIFEBIGBOOK.COM/LIFE_SUCCESS_WHEEL

YOUR BUSINESS WHEEL

You can use this tool for both your personal goals and for your business goals. Let's say you have business categories for Sales, Marketing, Operations, Special Projects, Leads, Consultations, Customer Service, or whatever applies to your business model. This allows you to track both your activity and your achievements.

The goal with this tool is to connect the dots and pull everything together in one place. It's easy to get lost in the weeds when you have all these goals and all these things you need to do to move the needle on your business. It's not about getting

> IT'S NOT ABOUT GETTING EVERYTHING TO A PERFECT TEN. IT'S ABOUT WHAT I CAN DO THIS WEEK THAT WILL MOVE THE NEEDLE.

everything to a perfect ten. It's about what I can do this week that will move the needle.

Maybe you do need to work a couple of late nights this week. Then, you get to have a conversation with your spouse about that. If one of your goals for your spouse was to be in communication about things, you may need to create a time and space for that. So many families don't know how to facilitate these kinds of conversations. But if you include them in your plan, you will figure out a way to make it happen.

BUILDING YOUR PLAN

All of the tools in this book are components of my Life Success Binder. As you move through the book, you will start to accumulate and integrate a set of tools that you can use to catapult your life and your business to a level you never imagined possible. They help you *Do Life Big*. These tools give you what you need to be deliberate and purposeful on your road to success. But they also help keep you on track, day to day, as you deal with all those unexpected events. When you get overwhelmed by life, you can go to your binder for clarity. It's all there in black and white.

Don't write a goal down unless you really want to do it. If you're writing it down because it sounds good, just take it off your list. It won't motivate you. Only put what's important to you on your list because, if it's important to you, you will find a way to make it happen. If you put something on your list because it sounds impressive, or someone else told you it was

> DON'T WRITE A GOAL DOWN UNLESS YOU REALLY WANT TO DO IT. IF YOU'RE WRITING IT DOWN BECAUSE IT SOUNDS GOOD, JUST TAKE IT OFF YOUR LIST. IT WON'T MOTIVATE YOU. ONLY PUT WHAT'S IMPORTANT TO YOU ON YOUR LIST BECAUSE, IF IT'S IMPORTANT TO YOU, YOU WILL FIND A WAY TO MAKE IT HAPPEN.

important, it will have the opposite effect of what this whole process seeks to achieve.

When your destination is crystal clear, in focus, and in front of you, you can put all your energy towards it and your dreams will manifest into your reality.

PART TWO

YOUR BUSINESS PLAN

CHAPTER FIVE

YOUR BUSINESS PLAN

I didn't start out with a plan. My first steps in business were a mixture of divine guidance and sheer determination. The stage was set back in the seventh grade at Edgerton Christian School when the board decided in their infinite wisdom to split what they considered to be a very large class of seventy-two students in half, according to their grade point average. I was in the lower grade point average group and it didn't take us long to figure out that we were the "dumb class." We lived up to it by making our teachers miserable and taking the easiest courses we could.

I was the last of three boys in a family of six children living on a dairy farm. By the time I got into high school, I knew I didn't want to farm, and neither did any of my siblings. So, when my dad sold the farm, I started to wonder, "What am I going to do?" My older siblings had all gone to college, but because I was part of the "dumb class" in school, I automatically assumed I was not college material and that maybe a vocational school would be more appropriate. I briefly contemplated going into automotive body repair. But one day, when I was in junior high, my dad and I were driving down the street in Sioux Falls and we passed the barber college.

I said, "Let's check that out," and he pulled into the parking lot. I had never been to a barber in my life. My mom had always cut my hair.

I went into the barber college and found out it was a nine-month course and it cost $950. So, I gave them a deposit. The next year, I was in a physiology class and my teacher, Mr. Hoekstra said, "What are you doing here?" implying that this was for smarter people than me. I said, "I'm going to the barber college and I need a physiology class." As it happened, Cheryln was also in that class. She was always in the smart class, but as it turned out, with that little bit of competition, my grades were just as good as hers.

MY BUSINESS STORY

When I graduated high school, I got the standard family gift of a suitcase. With six kids, I guess that was a symbol of something. So, the next morning, I got in the car and drove to Sioux Falls. One week later, on June first, I started barber college. Cheryln and I got married in December. When I got out of college in March, I was fortunate enough to find a job with a leading men's styling salon in town. The Vietnam war was ending and the long hair styles of the '60s and early '70s were transitioning into men discovering shorter hair cuts, hairspray and blow dryers. I worked there for a year, then the manager, Bob Christensen, opened his own men's styling shop and I went to work for him for three years.

I contemplated getting out of the business because I thought I wasn't making enough money. But then, a man who owned a small barber shop down the street called me and asked if I wanted to buy his business. It was a one-chair shop and I told him I wasn't interested. He called a second time, so I asked him how much he wanted for it and he said $1,500. I went to the bank and got a loan for $2,500, gave him a $1,500 check and I was in business. I didn't care how many customers he had. There was no non-compete. I just gave him a check and changed the name of the shop to Virg's Hair Design.

That weekend, I called all my previous customers on the phone and told them what I was doing. I had a clientele of about 200 customers, so when I opened up on the first Monday morning in March, I was booked. It's kind of ironic, because I started with 200 clients in 1976, and then in 1994, I sent 200 clients a letter saying we were no longer going to be doing hair cutting and hair styling for anyone that was not a hair replacement client.

I WENT TO THE BANK AND GOT A LOAN FOR $2,500, GAVE HIM A $1,500 CHECK AND I WAS IN BUSINESS.

By June of 1976, I hired my first employee, a guy right out of barber college. He worked for me for about six weeks. I bought a stereo from him and installed it in the shop so we would have music. One day, two police officers walked into the shop and asked for this guy by name. I pointed over to him and they arrested him on the spot for stealing stereos and CB radios. I didn't tell them about the radio behind my ceiling panel. But I went down to the jail that night and brought his tools to him and said, "I guess this is not going to work out." Next, I hired Cindy, who was there for about three years, then I hired a second barber stylist.

That first shop was about 400 square feet, with two chairs. When our business started to grow, I told the landlord, Mr. Ed Eastwald, I needed more space. There was a little cosmetic shop next door that was also about 400 square feet. I was paying $175 a month rent, so I said, "I'll give you $400 a month if we can take the wall down and I can have both spots." He agreed and then I had room for three chairs and a little office space. That was about the time we started doing more and more hair replacement work. I was able to create a private room for that, too.

I learned a major life lesson in those early years. I had several very good friends as clients who were movers and shakers in the city. They were visionaries and big business people and I would pick their brains when they came in for a haircut. Charlie Kearns was telling me about a new development on South Minnesota Avenue. It was a business center run like a condo. You could buy a 1,200 square foot area and own it, versus renting, for about $90,000. I had it all lined up with my banker and, over lunch, the president of US Bank himself said we were good to go. All he needed was a financial statement.

As I put that financial statement together, I realized I had done something not too smart. The previous year, I had skimmed about $10,000 off the top of the business that I didn't report. In a cash business like hair cutting, that's not too difficult to do. When the bank looked at my financial statement, they said I didn't have enough revenue to make the loan. I was about $10,000 short. That was a life lesson. In my presentations to people in this industry, I love to tell that story because the number one rule for being a successful business is, "Never steal from yourself."

We stayed in the old building until about 1990 when one of my clients built a new building on 26th Street. After sixteen years downtown, that was a big move away from our regular business focused clientele. But it was a much larger 1,200 square foot space in the brand new Ten Cate building, so we made the move. This was around the time we decided to become a full-time hair restoration salon.

After my daughter Sara graduated from beauty school, I encouraged her to go work somewhere else for a year before coming to work for us. After working somewhere else for eight months, that's when we fired all our old clients and went to just hair replacement. I had one employee leave, so I called Sara up and convinced her to come work with us before her year was up. She was with us for two years until she got married to Jeremy, who had one more year at the University of Minneapolis. When she left to go to Minneapolis, I thought that was the end of the world.

WHEN I SHARED THE LETTER WITH HER IT WAS BOTH AN EMOTIONAL MOMENT OF ME SHARING MY HEART AND A GOAL BEING FULFILLED FOR ME.

I was working with a coach at that time who suggested I write Sara a letter and put it away. In that letter, I stated what she meant to me and what she meant to the business and how I would love to have her come back, but she had to live her own life and do what she wanted to do. I added, if she did come back, our business would be great. And if she didn't, we would be all right, and so would she. About two years later, they moved back to

Sioux Falls and I gave her the letter. I wrote the letter as a goal and desire for myself while at the same time understanding that Sara had to live her own life and do what was best for her and Jeremy. When I shared the letter with her it was both an emotional moment of me sharing my heart and a goal being fulfilled for me.

The next six years were a period of steady growth. I measured my business by how many hair pieces I sold. When I would go to meetings for training, I'd ask other people how many hairpieces they sold. Many of them would lie with comments like, "Yeah, thousands. I'm so busy!" The more I talked to people, the closer I got to the truth. At that time, we had part of the top floor of the Ten Cate building. There was no room to store our inventory of hair, so we were using a small mechanical room. One employee had quit, so I didn't replace her. I was down to myself and one other employee. In 1997 Sara came to work with us again, and she brought her roommate to work with us because the business was growing. That same year, we doubled down on our growth goals.

When we moved into the Ten Cate building in the early 1990s, a friend of mine, Gene Van Kekerix, who was a CPA in that same building, suggested that we buy a piece of land across the street, and we did. The idea was to just keep making payments and get it paid off. Once we committed to the land, we built a new building the same year. We went from 1,200 square feet to 1,500 square feet, taking over half of the main level of the new building. It was not a big change, but we were able to set it up with private rooms that were a better fit for our business model.

After we built the new building, the lot next door came up for sale. We decided to buy that, just so we could control what went in there. We paid six dollars per square foot for that land and in 2001, Virg DeJongh became a third partner and we were able to build another building. I remember the day we signed the loan papers. It was September 11, 2001. We were scared. We moved our business into the lower level of the new building giving us 3,000 square feet. We thought that was huge, but we were soon looking for more space because our business had expanded into surgical hair transplants, working with a doctor who would come to Sioux Falls once a month.

By 2011, we needed more space to accommodate the transplant business. My partners bought me out of the building we built in 2001 and I bought them out of the building we built in 1997. This would give us the entire building using both floors and 6,000 square feet of space. On Friday, December 3rd of 2011, we found out Cheryln had cancer. The following Monday, December 6th, we started gutting the building and everyone was saying, "Are you sure you want to go through with this?" It was a big deal. We had two tenants that we had paid to leave, the contracts were signed, and at that point, there was no turning back.

Earlier in 2011, we began having discussions with Sara about taking over the business. First, we sat down with our lawyer, Sara and Jeremy, and Nathan and Holly. Cheryln and I laid everything out, showing them the value of everything we had and letting them know that we were starting to look at a succession plan. I wanted to give Nathan the opportunity to be a part of the business or to at least think about the possibility and have the conversation. At the time, he was in the pharmaceutical business and doing very well. Our business was very hands-on and it was hard for me to figure out a business model that would allow Nathan and Sara to be partners. But as it has grown, I realized, he could have been a part of it if he had wanted it. But I think it was God's plan that it didn't work out that way. I think it's better for our family that they are both doing what they are doing. God navigated us through that situation.

> WE HAD TWO TENANTS THAT WE HAD PAID TO LEAVE, THE CONTRACTS WERE SIGNED, AND AT THAT POINT, THERE WAS NO TURNING BACK.

Throughout this period of growth, we went from being Virg's Hair Design in 1976, to Virg's Hair Replacement in 1997, to Christoffels and Company around 2000. That's when we started talking about the succession plan. We wanted the company to be bigger than just Virg. Then, ultimately, we rebranded the company as Christoffels Hair Restoration in 2016.

In 2003, we received some amazing recognition. A publication called The National Hair Journal, a professional publication of the hair restoration business, used to name a Salon of the Year annually. In 2003, Christoffels was named the number one salon. The number two salon was in Asia. This was especially an honor because we were in Sioux Falls, South Dakota, the least populated area of any other salon in the running.

People sometimes tell me I'm lucky because we have no competition in town. But the other side of that is, we are the only ones in town telling that story. If you go to a big city that has a Hair Club for Men and several other hair replacement studios, they're all advertising the message that it's okay to do something about your hair loss. Here in Sioux Falls, we're the only ones telling that story and getting that message out there.

We always had a plan. And as we grew, we continually updated our plan, which enabled us to embrace new opportunities that showed up.

MY BUSINESS PLAN

I remember when I learned about the power of a business plan. In the early 1990s, I was working with my first business coach from Michael E. Gerber Companies. I had read the book *The E Myth* by Michael E. Gerber and contacted them for coaching. That was when I realized I needed to figure out how to write a business plan. That association didn't last a long time, but it opened my eyes to a lot of opportunities. Throughout my career, there were three key moments that really shaped how and why I created my Life Success Binder, which served me very well as my functioning buisness plan, both strategic and tactical.

The first key moment was when I started advertising in the 1980s. At first, I met with the people at KSFY-TV and ran ads without any plan. After attending a lot of seminars on business, I realized, I'm not a marketing guy. I know plenty about hair, but I needed to hire

THROUGHOUT MY CAREER, THERE WERE THREE KEY MOMENTS THAT REALLY SHAPED HOW AND WHY I CREATED MY LIFE SUCCESS BINDER, WHICH SERVED ME VERY WELL AS MY FUNCTIONING BUSINESS PLAN, BOTH STRATEGIC AND TACTICAL.

a professional to help me with marketing. So, I hired a company out of North Carolina, Barbara Goldstien from Media Power, who worked with a lot of other studios like ours. That's when I learned the importance of tracking my ROI (return on investment); how much I spent on TV, radio, Yellow Pages, and newspapers, and figuring out which ones were most effective.

I tracked how many leads came in from each ad, how many of those leads turned into consultations, and how many of those consultations turned into sales. I did a deep dive on that because we spent a lot of money on ads. That was the very beginning of really developing my Life Success Binder.

The next key thing I did was to write down the six things I value most, so I could share that with my staff. I needed a place to put my Values Statement, so it went right into this binder. Next, our whole staff designed a Mission Statement, which also went into the binder. I felt like my staff was an extension of me. How they communicated with a client was a reflection of me and my values. It was important to me that my staff understood and worked according to our core values and our mission statement. So, we started having monthly meetings to make sure that got communicated.

Along with that, we started doing a better job of goal setting, which was the core of our business plan. I broke it down into revenue, sales, marketing, administrative projects, and our top three priorities. I kept track of all that in the binder and looked at it against the balance sheet every month. By doing that, we were able to fine tune our financial report to reflect all the different income sources, from haircut services, to men's hair sales, women's hair sales, and other products. I could see where the biggest shares of revenue were coming from, by percentages. If our retail sales were down, we could decide to run a promotion. And we always shared our numbers, at least the percentages, with the staff. Our marketing people gave us a digital report at the end of every month, which allowed us to get more sophisticated in our ad spending.

I KEPT TRACK OF ALL THAT IN THE BINDER AND LOOKED AT IT AGAINST THE BALANCE SHEET EVERY MONTH.

Every Monday morning, I would look at all our goals for the year, broken down by month. I could instantly see what I needed to do that month in terms of how much revenue, how many leads, how many consults, and how many sales.

The third key moment was when Cheryln got cancer. I was no longer working with clients, I was just running the business. So, this binder had a huge impact on my ability to work *on* the business and not *in* the business and to keep the business on track. It helped me know where I needed to spend my time, because I was gone a lot. Sara and I would sit down every couple of weeks and go over these numbers. This binder is what I took to the hospital when Cheryln was having infusions. I'd look at these numbers and analyze if we were on track or off track. Sara was doing the day to day operations, but when we got ready to transition the business, it didn't take long for her to figure all this out.

Your business plan becomes essential when you want to grow intentionally. That's when you start to track your numbers. Then, when you start to build a team, you can use it to communicate your values. And when stuff hits the fan and life doesn't go your way and you need to know exactly what you need to do to be most effective, your business plan will be your rock. Having a plan like this builds strength in the business so you can run it without being there.

KEY ELEMENTS OF YOUR BUSINESS PLAN

VALUES:
What do you value in your business? When you walk through the door of your business, what do you value the most? What do you want your customers to see, hear, feel, smell, and say? What do you want them to experience? If you don't actively decide what those elements are, then write them

YOUR BUSINESS PLAN BECOMES ESSENTIAL WHEN YOU WANT TO GROW INTENTIONALLY. THAT'S WHEN YOU START TO TRACK YOUR NUMBERS. THEN, WHEN YOU START TO BUILD A TEAM, YOU CAN USE IT TO COMMUNICATE YOUR VALUES.

down and communicate them to your employees, they are probably not going to happen. As your business is growing and bringing in more people, your staff needs to know what you value and exactly what that looks like. Make your values duplicable and transferable.

———— THINGS I VALUE MOST ——— ✂ —

WWW.DOLIFEBIGBOOK.COM/VALUES

MISSION STATEMENT:

Who are you and what do you do? Our mission statement says,

"WITH PASSION AND INTEGRITY, WE RESTORE YOUR SELF ASSURANCE. WE LEAD THE INDUSTRY WITH OUR CONSISTENT QUALITY, AND INNOVATION. YOU WILL EXPERIENCE OUR TOTAL COMMITMENT TO YOUR TRANSFORMATION."

That sounds like a lot, but it speaks to who we are. We have a passion for what we do. We operate with integrity. And we want to restore your self assurance. We are industry leaders. We are consistent with quality and innovation. And when you walk in the door, you will experience our total commitment to your transformation. It's the whole picture of who we are. It's who we are, what we do, and what you're going to receive.

Creating our mission statement was a four-hour process. We closed our office for half a day, brought our entire staff to the Hilton Garden Inn's boardroom and had a good friend and mentor, Duane Salonen, lead us through this process. By the time we all left, everyone could say this statement without looking at it. Because our staff helped design it, they took ownership of it and had it memorized that day.

—————— MISSION STATEMENT —— ✂ —

WWW.DOLIFEBIGBOOK.COM/MISSION

GOALS:

Include both your personal and business goals in your Life Success Binder. These are your constant reminders. I used to meet with a business coach every month. He would look at all our goals and break them down to what we needed to accomplish that month.

For Personal Goals, I have physical, mental, spiritual, financial, relationships, family, and fun. For Business Goals I have revenue, sales, leads/consultations, marketing, staff training, and special projects. For each category, what do you want to do this month or this quarter? These will be things like working out four times, reading three books, journaling daily, studying the Book of Daniel, and holding regular meetings with staff and others, you get the idea.

I met with our advertising people monthly. They brought in their reports and we would go over those together to figure out how many leads came in, where they were spending money, and how much. I also generated a report every month with a breakdown of revenue by new client sales, existing client renewals, women's products sales, men's products sales, men's and women's hair sales, treatment programs, transplants, and no shows.

PROFIT AND LOSS STATEMENT:

We always looked at our year over year Profit and Loss by month. For instance, we looked at what we did in February and March of 2018 versus February and March of 2019.

TRACKING:

I always wanted to know every detail, not just the revenue, but the cost of sales, and cost per lead, so I could track that back to KPIs (Key Performance Indicators). This creates a story that helps you make meaning of the numbers, so you know what leverage you need to work on.

The big assessment happened at the end of the year, going through the entire budget. I have a sheet for my advertising evaluation report that includes total advertising dollars, total men's leads, total women's leads, cost per lead, cost per sale, and return on investment at the bottom. Being able to see if I'm spending too much or getting a good return is so valuable.

Having sales reports and marketing reports to look back on is great, but they also help you create an investment plan for the next year.

If you are just getting started in your business and all of this is a little overwhelming, you want to focus on the primary elements. You have to start with your *why*. Your *why* is your purpose or reason you are willing to sacrifice your effort to achieve these outcomes. What are you trying to do? What do you want to achieve? This is where I regret not having taken any business classes. Maybe it wouldn't have taken me forty-seven years to figure out a system that worked for me.

The latest statistics show that 50% of new businesses fail by their fifth year. If you're starting a new business, you want to do it right. One of the best ways to do that is to follow a proven plan that will keep you on track through all the expected and unexpected things that come up daily. You want to be able to go to the bank and get loans when you need them. You want to be able to show them your passion, your why, your goals, and your numbers.

> I ALWAYS WANTED TO KNOW EVERY DETAIL, NOT JUST THE REVENUE, BUT THE COST OF SALES, AND COST PER LEAD, SO I COULD TRACK THAT BACK TO KPIS (KEY PERFORMANCE INDICATORS). THIS CREATES A STORY THAT HELPS YOU MAKE MEANING OF THE NUMBERS, SO YOU KNOW WHAT LEVERAGE YOU NEED TO WORK ON.

Your Life Success Binder holds everything in one place and keeps you accountable to what you say you want. It's your measuring tool. And it's real data. The pages you need to write up and print out to get your business operational are:

- **Your Values**
- **Your Mission Statement**
- **Annual Goals Tracker**
- **Monthly Life Success Scorecard**

- **KPIs needed to run your business – one page for each item you want to track**
- **Job Descriptions for key employees**

Go back to Chapters Two and Three, print out those sheets and start filling them out. Then, assemble your *Key Performance Indicators*. Put them all into your binder. Keep that binder on your desk and review it every Monday, preferably with your spouse. As you move through it, you will own it and hone it. But this is your starting point.

Some people just want to get operational. Others will want to hire a coach to help them master their business plan so they can *Do Life Big*. At the end of this book, you will find options for taking your skills to the next level.

CHAPTER SIX

CREATING YOUR EXCEPTIONAL CUSTOMER EXPERIENCE

No matter what kind of business you have, when your customer enters, (even if it's online), they are going to have an experience. The experience that customer has can make or break your business. This is such a big deal that there are many books focusing solely on customer experience. In the book, *The Experience Economy*, the authors clearly state that, "Future economic growth lies in the value of experiences and transformations—goods and services are no longer enough." Many of the customer service things we do are ideas borrowed from John R. Dijulius III in his book *The Secret Service*.

In this chapter, you will learn how and why you need to create a personal experience for your customers that will become the reason everyone talks about your business, the reason your business grows, and what becomes the soul of your business.

At Christoffels Hair Restoration, we always strive to give our clients a Ritz-Carlton level experience. In our industry, privacy is a big thing. It's the kind of business no one really wants to visit. The office is designed so that, when you walk in, a bunch of people are not sitting in a group, waiting. If you're coming in for the first time, you will walk right to the front desk, be greeted by the receptionist, and have your appointment confirmed. Then, she will immediately take you to a private consultation room, offer you a beverage, and close the door so you can wait in private for the consultant.

We have two consultation rooms. One has four chairs and a high-top table. It's a comfortable setting to have a discussion and look at photos. The other room has big comfortable chairs and a TV on the wall for showing pictures, and for scanning. Our first order of business is to find out what clients' needs are. We like to say, our business is event driven, so we also want to find out what's driving this now. It's usually a marriage, a divorce, an anniversary, a class reunion, or something that causes people to decide they need to finally do something about their hair loss.

IT'S IMPORTANT TO KNOW ALL THE TOUCH POINTS IN YOUR BUSINESS, FROM THE TIME THEY CALL, TO THE MOMENT THEY WALK IN THE FRONT DOOR, TO HOW THE RECEPTIONIST GREETS THEM, AND THEN BRINGS THEM TO A ROOM. WE THINK OF OUR BUSINESS AS BEING A THEATER PERFORMANCE. EVERYTHING IS ORCHESTRATED.

Once they become a client, we want them to have that family feeling. When they come in again, the receptionist takes them back. We have ten private rooms and eight stylists, so clients can all receive their service behind closed doors. Very few people ever see each other coming or going.

It's important to know all the touch points in your business, from the time they call, to the moment they walk in the front door, to how the receptionist greets them, and then brings them to a room. We think of our business as being a theater performance. Everything is orchestrated.

We even have a back room that we call the backstage. That's where we get ready for the show. When you walk into that room with a client, you are on stage and you do your performance, dressed to impress.

The feedback we receive matches our intention. The comments are usually about our professionalism, privacy, and hands on approach. Also, that the experience is comfortable and first class. I remember hosting the bi-annual meeting for Transitions, our trade organization, here in Sioux Falls one year. We bussed all the members over to our studio for a tour and they couldn't believe this place was in Sioux Falls, South Dakota. One person said, "Gosh, my house isn't this nice." Another guy said, "I'm just going to go home and burn my place down."

I think it's important for us to have a first-class place because we sell an expensive product and people make a big commitment to do it. It's like going to the Audi dealership to have your car serviced. The salesmen all have on ties with a sport coat or a suit. It sends a message. This is going to cost me some money, but I'm getting a great product and the very best service.

Our biggest source of new clients now is referrals, which is remarkable because we always considered ourselves to be in the whisper business. It's not something you're going to tell your buddies about. Women will share that information more than men. For the men who know me, if they have a friend who's struggling with hair loss, they will say, "You need to go see Virg." Of course, now they say, "You need to go see Sara." That's high trust.

We also ask for evaluations from the people we serve and those are almost always good. They love the personal touch. And our technicians make people feel welcomed and comfortable. But the most satisfying thing is to see the lift in a client's self-confidence, self-esteem, and self-love. You literally see people come in without hair, and you do some

YOU ALSO WANT TO CREATE A POSITIVE EXPERIENCE FOR YOUR TEAM. I WANT MY TEAM TO FEEL LIKE THEY ARE PART OF SOMETHING GREAT, THAT THEY ARE CHANGING PEOPLE'S LIVES, AND HAVING AN IMPACT.

type of hair restoration and their face goes from frowning and unhappy to a big cheeky smile.

The customer experience that we create for our clients sets us apart from other hair replacement studios. We know this because some of our clients go to warmer locations for the winter. And when they come back, they let us know how happy they are to be back because the experience in our studio is different. That tells me they really appreciate it and I think they see value for their dollar.

The Experience Economy goes beyond just clients. You also want to create a positive experience for your team. I want my team to feel like they are part of something great, that they are changing people's lives, and having an impact. It's not unusual for our stylists doing someone's hair for the first time to get a big hug, just because the customer feels so good about what they did and the transformation it made in their life.

ELEMENTS OF EXCEPTIONAL CUSTOMER EXPERIENCE

One of the fundamental requirements for creating a memorable customer experience is first having a really intimate understanding of your customer. If you're going to build an experience that matters to people, you need to know what they value. Little things make a huge difference. We had one customer who always wanted a Diet Coke on ice. So, whenever he came in, the technician would have a Diet Coke on ice waiting for him. It seems like a stupid little thing, but people love knowing that someone went out of their way to do something like that just for them. Cleanliness is another thing people really appreciate. These are not huge things. They just require attention to details, big and small.

Once you understand your customer, the three most powerful elements for crafting your unique customer experience are:

- Be welcoming
- Provide over-the-top customer service
- Do the unexpected

CREATING *YOUR* EXCEPTIONAL CUSTOMER EXPERIENCE

There are certain steps you need to go through to start to create and implement your exceptional customer experience. To do anything well, there's only ever one place to start: evaluation.

PHYSICAL PRESENTATION

You need to evaluate what you have right now. Start with the physical. What does your facility look like? What does your customer encounter when they walk into your business? When they walk in, do they see hair in the corners? Busted woodwork? Chipped paint? Are your employees standing around talking to each other and ignoring you? Look at every little thing through the eyes of your customer.

What kind of atmosphere have you created? Is it clean or dirty? Organized or messy? Loud or quiet? Do you, or does anyone, greet your customer? What does that look like? Some major blunders include uncleanliness, disrepair, bad lighting, unkempt staff, and not acknowledging people when they arrive.

> WHAT KIND OF ATMOSPHERE HAVE YOU CREATED? IS IT CLEAN OR DIRTY? ORGANIZED OR MESSY? LOUD OR QUIET? DO YOU, OR DOES ANYONE, GREET YOUR CUSTOMER? WHAT DOES THAT LOOK LIKE?

One of the most underrated positions in many businesses is the person who answers your phone. I can't tell you how many places I've called and I just wanted to hang up. Your receptionist position should not be a revolving door of disrespected and disrespectful people. If you think this is a great place to cut costs, think again. This person is the voice of your company.

You, and your employees, should also look the part for what you're selling. We were in the appearance business, so we really had to present ourselves well. You should look like what your client wants to look like.

TOUCH POINTS

Do an inventory of all the points of contact you currently have with your clients and brainstorm all the ways you can interact with them in positive ways. This could include reminder calls for appointments, follow up calls after appointments, and automatically rebooking regular customers. We have a client who comes in every three weeks at a set time he likes. When he leaves, we hand him a card with his next appointment time on it. We've also done the unexpected, like sending out sympathy cards when we know someone in their family has died. We send out birthday cards. And, when we have a new female client, we get a nice flower arrangement to give her when she leaves after her first visit.

Try to anticipate your clients' needs. With hair replacement, we understood that privacy was important to our clients. Be aware that your client may be nervous about shopping for something unfamiliar. You need to respect that. What would make them feel good? What could you do for them without them having to ask for it? What can they get at your establishment that they can't get anyplace else? Try to discover what trips their triggers and minimize those things.

If you work one-on-one with people, find a way to remember anything important about your clients. It may be their birthday, something about their family, or their kids, or their job. Find out what they like to talk about.

Sit down and write up all the touchpoints your business has with your clients. Map them out by pre-visit, during their visit, and post-visit. Then, tackle them one at a time, figuring out how to best 'wow' your clients. You can do this for an online business, as well as a physical business. Just go online and notice every step your customer has to go through to do business with you. Then, address and refine each of those steps.

FEEDBACK

The last part of evaluation is asking for feedback. You have to create an atmosphere where your clients are comfortable giving you feedback. Sometimes, business owners can be afraid to open that door because they think they're asking for trouble. They keep that door shut, but in doing so, they are losing a real opportunity to shine. Sometimes people talk more about how great you are after you've gone out of your way to fix a mistake than if everything had gone perfectly. Ask your customers how your product is working for them. Did they like what they got last time? Do we need to make any changes or adjustments? What can we do better? What would you like to have happen? Don't take anything for granted.

There are many ways to implement feedback. You can do it through intentional conversation, forms, or surveys. We talk about these things in our staff meetings. How are we doing? Has anyone seen anything we need to address? We also police each other. If I see a client at the front counter with hair on their shoulders, they're going back in the room. That's unacceptable. These are all points of excellence that we work on constantly.

When you, as the business owner, take the time to look at what your clients actually see and experience, and you evaluate every one of those steps, you can come up with a great customer experience.

> WHEN YOU, AS THE BUSINESS OWNER, TAKE THE TIME TO LOOK AT WHAT YOUR CLIENTS ACTUALLY SEE AND EXPERIENCE, AND YOU EVALUATE EVERY ONE OF THOSE STEPS, YOU CAN COME UP WITH A GREAT CUSTOMER EXPERIENCE.

CHAPTER SEVEN
PHASES OF GROWTH AND TRANSITION

In every stage of the growth and transition of my business, which I outlined in Chapter Five, I had to identify, learn from, and leave behind pieces of my business and myself to make way for the next stage of growth and transition. Every company that is growing, or wants to grow, will have to do the same thing. You will reach points of no return where you are either going to sink or swim. I like to describe these moments as "burning the ships."

Burning the ships is about commitment. You throw away the crutches and the safety net. You abandon your comfort zone and strike out into new territory. You sink or you swim. You give yourself no other options. This may sound brutal, but it's necessary. You can't move forward by hanging onto the past. It's true in so much of life, but especially so in business.

If you're really sincere, and you've thought, prayed, and deliberated for a long time, then you're probably ready to move forward. To be a success, you have to take chances. And a lot of the time, you just figure it out as you go. You want to be as resourceful as you can to minimize any potential damage, of course. But you can't be thinking about how you can go backwards if it doesn't work out. For me, going back always felt like failing. Your old thoughts, ideas, and identity can detract from your next level of influence and impact in the world.

VIRG THE BARBER

My first growth phase was my first year as a barber working for a very successful men's hair styling salon. After that first year, one of the guys I worked with decided to open his own salon. I had to decide, do I go with him? Or do I stay where I'm comfortable? I had to burn that first ship to move to my next phase of growth.

VIRG'S HAIR DESIGN

After three years at the new place, I had an opportunity to go out on my own. I had been an employee for four years. As limited as it was, it was still a secure job. I was gaining experience, learning how to cut hair, and I was learning the business. I worked on a percentage basis, but I always knew there was more. The thought had crossed my mind that, if I owned the business, I could keep all the money, instead of just a percentage of what I was bringing in.

What I had to leave behind to step into Virg's Hair Design included education. If I had a question, or didn't know how to do something, there was always someone to ask at my job. And while it wasn't a guaranteed income, there was a steady client base coming in. I knew I had 200 regular clients, but the big risk was, would they follow me over to my new business? If they didn't come, that would severely impact my income. That was a tough decision.

Stepping out on my own, I would have to make my own decisions, but being able to keep all the revenue was a big deal for me. I was excited about the growth opportunities. I wasn't thinking about hairpieces at that time. I had done a few, but that wasn't foremost on my radar yet. I was more interested in creating a business with my own culture. For example, where I had been working, if you went into the waiting area, you would find a Playboy Magazine on the magazine rack. That wasn't the image or culture that I wanted to display. It was sort of an expected thing back then. But, I really wanted to do things my way. I wanted my business to be a class act and also a place where my faith would show through.

IF YOU'RE REALLY SINCERE, AND YOU'VE THOUGHT, PRAYED, AND DELIBERATED FOR A LONG TIME, THEN YOU'RE PROBABLY READY TO MOVE FORWARD. TO BE A SUCCESS, YOU HAVE TO TAKE CHANCES. AND A LOT OF THE TIME, YOU JUST FIGURE IT OUT AS YOU GO.

VIRG'S HAIR REPLACEMENT

After sixteen years of being downtown in a great location on 10th Street, which was a target rich environment for businessmen needing a haircut, we moved to the edge of town, away from our long-term clientele. Would they trade walking around the corner to get a haircut for getting in their car and driving out to 26th Street? That was a big risk.

This was about the same time that hair replacement started to become a bigger part of our business, so it seemed like a good time to change the name to include "hair replacement." What we were stepping into was the growth potential that would come with changing our image. We wanted to change our brand from just doing haircuts to doing hair replacement, as well. The name change opened the door to better capitalize on marketing and advertising. We needed the company name to reflect the new direction of our business. And now, it did.

To grow the hair replacement business, we started selling ladies' wigs, and getting into the medical market for women.

CHRISTOFFELS AND COMPANY

This was a big ship to burn. Going from Virg's Hair Replacement to Christoffels and Company meant dropping my first name and using my last name instead. The business was maturing and growing into a bigger vision of what we could be. This was when we sent out those letters telling our 200 haircut clients we were no longer doing traditional hair cutting and hair styling. The big risk was, haircuts represented a good portion of our income on an annual basis. Letting that go was a huge step that had been on our goals list for at least eight years. You could really see the flames from those burning boats!

When we moved from downtown, we knew we were going to lose some customers, but we also knew we wouldn't lose them all. But this time, we fired them all. We put all our eggs in one basket. If hair replacement sales were down a little, we couldn't make up that revenue with haircuts. There was no turning back. On the contrary, that change set us apart in our industry. People didn't say, "Oh, they're trying something new." They said, "Oh, this is no longer a haircut place. It's hair replacement. That's all they do." That exclusivity positioned us as the experts, not just something we did as a side hustle.

The new brand really launched us as a noticeable entity in the world of hair replacement, not just in Sioux Falls, but all around. We had clients from Canada whose friends couldn't believe they had that great work done in Sioux Falls.

Another goal of becoming Christoffels and Company was to make the business more inclusive of Sara. She wasn't the owner yet, but that was the plan. I also think it gave the impression of being bigger than just a hairstyling salon. We were stepping into a bigger vision, a bigger identity, and a bigger future.

It also represented a bigger commitment to the business and getting deeper into the business plan. As we stepped into this new business model, we started to put our plans into action.

CHRISTOFFELS HAIR RESTORATION

As Sara started buying the business and taking more ownership of it, we started to restructure the business. We wrote up job descriptions for every staff member. We identified a new manager position, and selected one of the current staff to fill that position.

We put a lot of emphasis on the importance of our business plan. We already had our mission statement, goals, and tracking documents, but defining roles and job descriptions was a key step as Sara started moving into more of a leadership position.

Another thing we did at that time was update our logo. It had been a fancy, scrolling C&C. We hired a new marketing company and one of their suggestions was to make our image more contemporary.

I remember having a meeting with the staff where everyone had sticky notes. We all wrote down everything we did in the business. Staff were responsible for cutting hair, greeting customers, checking customers out, cleaning hair, and various other jobs. We put it all on the wall and that's when I realized I was doing the same things. After looking at that list, we asked the staff, what is on Virg's list that you guys can do? One by one, all of those jobs disappeared from my list, except for one: running the business. That was my eye opener. I needed to step away from being the guy behind the chair and become the president or CEO who worked *on* the business, instead of *in* the business.

One of the hardest things to leave behind at this stage was being that guy behind the chair. I had always been very hands on with my clients. I enjoyed that, but you sometimes get clients who think you're God and the only one who can help them. Ironically, this was around the timeframe when Cheryln got sick. Stepping away from that

> WE PUT A LOT OF EMPHASIS ON THE IMPORTANCE OF OUR BUSINESS PLAN. WE ALREADY HAD OUR MISSION STATEMENT, GOALS, AND TRACKING DOCUMENTS, BUT DEFINING ROLES AND JOB DESCRIPTIONS WAS A KEY STEP.

became easier because I just wasn't able to be there. Those clients just had to start going to other stylists and most of them simply adopted the change.

However, I had one client who came in about four times a year. He only wanted me to do his hair and I always thought it was just easier to do it than argue with him. After I stepped away from being behind the chair, I ran into him in town. He complained that, "It's not the same, Virg, when you don't do my hair." Somebody else did it and he didn't like it. So, I said, "I'll talk to Sara." Well, he didn't come back. The temptation with something like that is to get too emotionally involved. When you own a business, your emotions have to be under control. If you make decisions by your emotions, you get stuck. Your ego gets in the way and you throw gas on the fire. Yes, I want happy customers, but I recognize, I'm not going to satisfy everyone. Everybody has different expectations and I try my best to figure out what those are. But sometimes, you just have to walk away.

> IF YOU ARE STRUGGLING WITH THE IDEA OF BURNING SOME SHIPS TO MOVE FORWARD IN YOUR BUSINESS, JUST KNOW THAT IT DOESN'T HAVE TO BE COMPLICATED. WHAT DO YOU WANT TO BE? WHAT DO YOU WANT TO DO? HOW DO YOU WANT TO SPEND YOUR TIME?

If you are struggling with the idea of burning some ships to move forward in your business, just know that it doesn't have to be complicated. What do you want to be? What do you want to do? How do you want to spend your time? Go back to your vision. Revisit your goals and your mission and ask yourself what role you want to play in that. What do you have to do to make your vision a reality? Sit down and write out all the tasks you're doing.

If you're mopping the floor at night, vacuuming, calling to make appointments, and you don't have time to focus on your business, then that stuff has to go away. You either have to get rid of it or find someone else to do it. You have to ask yourself, if your time is worth $200 an hour, why are you doing a $15 an hour job?

Who do you want to be in your business? What's the role you want to play long term? Do you want to be the rainmaker or the overseer? I think it's important for every business owner to recognize where their time is best spent, for the sake of the growth, development, and longevity of the business.

Burning your ships is about making decisions and not second guessing yourself. People spend too much time visiting old places. When you burn the ships, there's no place to go. There's no parachute. You're burning your options. This is a common point of failure for many business owners because it's comfortable to go back to what's familiar. Once your business is growing, that's when it's important to determine your role and eliminate or delegate the things you don't want to do.

> BURNING YOUR SHIPS IS ABOUT MAKING DECISIONS AND NOT SECOND GUESSING YOURSELF. PEOPLE SPEND TOO MUCH TIME VISITING OLD PLACES. WHEN YOU BURN THE SHIPS, THERE'S NO PLACE TO GO.

PART THREE

YOUR LEGACY PLAN

CHAPTER EIGHT
YOUR BUSINESS SUCCESSION PLAN

Succession begins when you give your *business someday* a date. My process started in 2010.

When you begin thinking about an exit strategy, you want to be methodical. The most important things you can do are to recognize the importance of documentation and have your business in a place where it doesn't depend on you. In my case, I had to remove myself as the face of the business, putting more emphasis on the business, and less on me. This is also when we took our Life Success Binder to the next level.

When you start preparing your business for sale, you never know who might buy it. Once the decision was made that my daughter Sara would be the buyer, it cleared up that part for me. I knew who was going to buy it, and that was a gift. But I also wanted to make her successful. Having everything documented and going through the process to lay out all the job descriptions, including mine and Sara's, made the whole process become more real. We really put wheels under it.

When my role changed, I saw myself more as a business owner and an entrepreneur, running the business instead of working in it. And I felt that made the business stronger. The more independent of me the business became, the stronger the business got because it could sustain itself. It no longer depended on me showing up every day to do all the things that needed to get done. All those key customer touch points we talked about were no longer things I had to do myself. I had worked on that for a long time and, finally, I knew those things would get done whether I was there or not.

> THE MORE INDEPENDENT OF ME THE BUSINESS BECAME, THE STRONGER THE BUSINESS GOT BECAUSE IT COULD SUSTAIN ITSELF. IT NO LONGER DEPENDED ON ME SHOWING UP EVERY DAY TO DO ALL THE THINGS THAT NEEDED TO GET DONE.

MY SUCCESSION PROCESS

Cheryln and I had created a trust and we started the process by laying all of that out in front of our kids. We had the business evaluated and I wanted both of them, but especially Nathan, to know how and why the business was evaluated so that if he had a question about it, or wasn't comfortable with it, I wanted to know about it right then. I didn't want to be dead and have my kids challenge the plan we laid out. So, we were very transparent about everything.

Once it was decided that Sara was going to buy the business, we could focus on how we would do this. We had the help of an attorney and an accountant, but my first decision was, how soon did I want to start selling. We started selling the company in ten percent increments. In 2013, Sara went to the bank and got a loan to pay for the first ten percent. Two years later, she bought the second ten percent. At four years, she bought another ten percent. The plan was for her to pay the balance and take over at the end of 2019.

But, when Cheryln died, I was ready to be done. So, we knew in the middle of 2018 that Sara was going to take over at the end of that year. That last six months was more of a rehearsal as Sara was doing more of my role and getting Kayla up to speed, as the manager, on what she had been doing.

The day I walked out of that office for the last time, no longer the business owner, was pretty anticlimactic. I thought it was going to be a big deal. We had two lawyers who came over with all the paperwork drawn up. We signed the papers and it was done. It was around Christmas time and someone had sold us a case of what I called "relief." I poured myself a glass of wine and shared the rest with all the customers who were there that day. I got a picture of Sara and I with a glass of wine in her office and I said, "This is not the way I expected it to be." I had expected Cheryln and I to ride off into the sunset and live happily ever after. It was all good, I just didn't expect to be celebrating all by myself. I think it was kind of awkward for Sara, too.

> THE DAY I WALKED OUT OF THAT OFFICE FOR THE LAST TIME, NO LONGER THE BUSINESS OWNER, WAS PRETTY ANTICLIMACTIC.

Having an anticlimactic exit is not entirely bad. A smooth transition means you are leaving your business in a good situation, which so few business owners ever do. Many have to step back in, and it becomes a long drawn out process. I didn't want to be that guy. Sara and I had a kind of unspoken agreement that I was going to stay out of there for six months. She called a few times, and I helped her with some marketing, but she was totally ready to take over.

The only thing harder than getting into business is getting out. First of all, I recognize that Sara was a big gift. But Cheryln was a big part of the business, too. I feel like I got a thumbs up from Cheryln and a thumbs up from Sara. And I also felt that Nathan was OK with the transition.

Looking back over the whole thing, I think it took Sara about six months to fully transition into her new position as owner of the business. I really noticed it when she had her own Life Success Binder. In January, she called me and asked if I could come over and review what she was thinking about doing for marketing. As I sat down, she slipped her binder in front of me. I opened it up and there were her sales records and reports from advertising. That made everything so easy. Everything came full circle. It was a family business dream succession. And, of course, God was at the center of this, too.

> EVERYTHING CAME FULL CIRCLE. IT WAS A FAMILY BUSINESS DREAM SUCCESSION. AND, OF COURSE, GOD WAS AT THE CENTER OF THIS, TOO.

I still have my binder from 2018. That was the last business plan I put together for the company. I remember thinking for a moment, "I should update that." But then I remembered, no, I'm retired. A lot of people say that when they leave a business, they miss it. As fun as that business was for me, I truly feel like I've moved on to a different part of my life.

CREATING YOUR SUCCESSION PROCESS

You have to have a solid business model to have something to sell. You can't just say, here are some customers and here's how much money we make every year. To have a successful sale, if they want to continue to operate the business like you do, you need to have documentation of what you do, how you do it, and a list of the people who help you do it. You need to outline what your goals have been, what your achievements have been, and what your expectations are for the future. All of that helps to establish a value. And you may want to hire an outside entity to help you establish that value. One of the accountants at the firm we use is certified in business evaluation, so that's who we used.

We evaluated our business in a number of ways. One was, if we sold the business and I stayed on, the business would be worth more than if I sold the business and I left. It's also probably worth more to Sara because she can transition right into running the business and the clients are already comfortable with her. We also looked at the revenue. Then, we took all that into consideration. We took the high value and the low value and settled on an in between price. Then, we built in an escalator for increased revenue, since she was buying it over time. But in our case, we kept the price the same. Sara was there working with me to build the business. So, I felt it wouldn't be fair to escalate the price on something she helped to build.

It was important to us to establish the value of the business by the book; to make it completely fair and without emotion. That keeps family at the Thanksgiving table.

In addition to a real and fair price evaluation, you need to have something like a Life Success Binder because it's that business plan that sells. You can sell customers to anybody. But if you want to keep it as a business, you need to be able to state that this business, with this business model, and this revenue, is worth X. And if you take this business model and do exactly what we're doing, here's what you should make. This is what the return will be. If you're an entrepreneur, you could buy this business and, the way it's set up right now, it could run. You don't have to know anything about hair. That might make it easier, but on the other hand, it could make it harder because sometimes, you know too much. If you just know business, you can make it work.

YOU HAVE TO HAVE A SOLID BUSINESS MODEL TO HAVE SOMETHING TO SELL. YOU CAN'T JUST SAY, HERE ARE SOME CUSTOMERS AND HERE'S HOW MUCH MONEY WE MAKE EVERY YEAR. TO HAVE A SUCCESSFUL SALE, IF THEY WANT TO CONTINUE TO OPERATE THE BUSINESS LIKE YOU DO, YOU NEED TO HAVE DOCUMENTATION OF WHAT YOU DO, HOW YOU DO IT, AND A LIST OF THE PEOPLE WHO HELP YOU DO IT.

One of the regrets I have had in life is that I never had any business classes; I never went to business school. I'm not sure what difference that would have made, if any. I hired coaches along the way who were a big help. And the rest I learned by doing. I just feel blessed that, in the end, I had the mindset to see that I didn't have to run a scissor to run this business. The model is here. And I think that's how Sara sees it, too.

When I was in the process of leaving, and I was just there running the business, it was easy for staff to run up to me and ask me questions. I was very purposeful about saying, "Talk to Sara. I don't run this place anymore. I'm not the operations person. Talk to Sara."

Having a solid business model is the main ingredient in succession planning. If your business has not stressed keeping good records, has not excelled in customer service and cleanliness, and has not provided a special customer experience, when you quit, a large percentage of the customers are also going to leave.

If you do everything in this book over a fifteen-year period, you're going to have something you can actually sell. That is the American business dream. While you're doing life anyway, you might as well *Do Life Big*.

CHAPTER NINE
SOMEDAY STARTS TODAY

Cheryln and I had a warning that our life's *someday* was coming. We didn't know exactly when, but we knew it would be sooner, rather than later. We had time to plan. But we were also planning long before that. Sometimes, people die suddenly. If you're twenty or thirty years younger than me, maybe there's a lesson there. If something happens to you, you miss your someday. And whoever you leave behind, that becomes their someday.

It all comes back to your goals. What's really important to you? What do you want your life to look like? What do you want to leave behind? What message do you want to leave for your family? If you get wiped out tomorrow, what value and what comfort will you leave your loved ones?

TALK ABOUT IT

You can make all the plans in the world, but it doesn't mean things are going to end like you thought they would. Cheryln didn't leave this world the way she thought she would. But that doesn't mean you shouldn't talk about everything and make plans for everything. Cheryln and I talked about everything. She knew what was happening in the business. She knew what was going on with our family. She even made it very clear to our kids that they should not let me sell the lake house after she passed. She understood why that was important.

Don't just write your goals, put them in your binder, and never look at them again. Talk about what's important to you. Dream out loud. Together. Yes, everything can change in an instant. But it's much easier to turn a vehicle that's moving than it is to get something moving from a dead stop. I really don't even like that word "goals." It's so generic. I'm talking about creating a picture of the life you hope to have. What do you want it to look like and feel like? What are you working towards? Create that one big vision of how you want your life to work. Apply the balance wheel to it. Choose the categories of life that are most important to you and your family and fill in the objectives that you think will get you there. Sometimes we get there and sometimes we don't. That, too, is life. But we need to be ready. Whether it's business or your personal life, if something happens to you tomorrow, you need to have your ducks in a row. Plan for financial stability. Have options for your business, if that's valuable to you. It was to me. If something had happened to me five years ago, I would still want Sara to be in a place where she could keep that business going.

> YOU CAN MAKE ALL THE PLANS IN THE WORLD, BUT IT DOESN'T MEAN THINGS ARE GOING TO END LIKE YOU THOUGHT THEY WOULD.

When we got notice that our someday was coming, I was able to step back from the business and take the time necessary to spend with Cheryln. Sara was able to step in and help me to do that. We also had the time, which was a blessing, to fine tune and sharpen the business model so she could step in and take over. You can't wait. The day you start your business is not too soon to start thinking about what you would do if you were not going to be in this business anymore. Do I want to just shut the door? Or, do I want someone to take it over and run with it? It's never too soon to start planning and creating your exit strategy.

LEGACY

For me, legacy is about making a difference. When I think about my kids, my friends, and people who know me, I ask myself, have I made a difference in their lives? When I'm gone, will they think of me and say, "I'm better because I knew that person." Or, "I'm better because of what he brought to the table. I've benefited from knowing him."

When you start thinking, "*Someday*, I'd like to start a business," or "*Someday*, I'd like to sell this business," or any other goals you have, put a date on that. Start pulling that desire into reality by putting a timeline on it. Start writing it down. I wrote, talked about, and planned for having a hair restoration business for eight years before it actually happened. Pull the things that are valuable to you into your mentality and start living them now.

I have a few really good friends who have large businesses but are struggling to find a way out. They are older in age and love what they do. They have things in order as to who will get what after they die, but they have not been able to put together a clear plan to ensure the business will continue smoothly when they are gone. Legacy is about so much more than money. If you value what you've spent your life creating, why wouldn't you want to do everything in your power to ensure it continues after you're gone? Start now. Don't wait. You may not get your someday.

> FOR ME, LEGACY IS ABOUT MAKING A DIFFERENCE. WHEN I THINK ABOUT MY KIDS, MY FRIENDS, AND PEOPLE WHO KNOW ME, I ASK MYSELF, HAVE I MADE A DIFFERENCE IN THEIR LIVES? WHEN I'M GONE, WILL THEY THINK OF ME AND SAY, "I'M BETTER BECAUSE I KNEW THAT PERSON."

A NEW START

Cheryln left two very powerful messages for our family in the form of letters; one for me and one for our kids and grandkids. In her final letter to me, she talked about the encouragement I was to her and how she would be the angel by my side. Then, she said that I should get married again after she was gone.

LEGACY IS ABOUT SO MUCH MORE THAN MONEY. IF YOU VALUE WHAT YOU'VE SPENT YOUR LIFE CREATING, WHY WOULDN'T YOU WANT TO DO EVERYTHING IN YOUR POWER TO ENSURE IT CONTINUES AFTER YOU'RE GONE? START NOW. DON'T WAIT. YOU MAY NOT GET YOUR SOMEDAY.

Cheryln liked to tell the story of how her mom, who died of cancer, not only told her dad he should marry again, she even picked out the woman she wanted him to marry. They were at a dinner one night, close to the end, when this lady was walking across the room. Her mom pointed and said to Cheryln, "That's the woman I told Dad he should marry." He did, and they were married for fourteen years.

Cheryln graciously wrote that she wouldn't pick out who I should marry, like her mom did for her dad, but that I should take my time and find a Christian woman. So, I think I did the right thing. I'm not sure about taking the time. Cheryln died in February 2018 and Ann and I got married in June of 2019. I put that on Cheryln because she didn't exactly define what she meant by "take your time."

Ann and I met through a mutual friend who knew both Cheryln and I, as well as Ann and her husband. Ann lost her husband and had been alone for six years. I was only alone for a year and a half. It's been a new journey for both of us and our children, but that's part of continuing on with our lives. We are learning as we go. Ann was still working when we got married, so she retired a little quicker than she planned. She's a little younger than me, but I feel blessed to be able to love again.

The relationship I had with Cheryln was different from the relationship Ann had with Doug. So now that we are together, we both need to draw from those first marriage experiences and expectations to set new goals and dreams for a new relationship. Our vision is to focus on our family. To make time for our kids. To focus on building our relationship and to build a home together. We want to unify our lives and our families. I'm still trying to set that example because, again, I feel like people are watching us to see how we do this.

Ann and I have grieved together and openly talked a lot about Cheryln and Ann's first husband, Doug. He is still her children's dad and Cheryln is still my children's mom and those memories have not disappeared. We want to keep their memory alive for our kids and grandkids.

That first summer after Cheryln died, I spent time at the lake journaling. I was writing about building a bridge. I thought about going through the valley of the shadow of death and how I could either slug my way through the mud, or I could build a bridge to go over it. The way I built the bridge was with the pillars in my life. And the pillars in my life are the people around me. They are the hands that helped me build that bridge to get over the valley.

WALL OF GRATITUDE

Legacy is about your beginning, your middle, your end, and the people you gather around you. My story has always been about people; my family, friends, clients, employees, mentors and coaches. I've always had a coach. And I've always worked at bringing people around me.

I was never afraid to ask questions. I think there was a time when people thought I went to seminars for fun. But that was the only way I knew how

LEGACY IS ABOUT YOUR BEGINNING, YOUR MIDDLE, YOUR END, AND THE PEOPLE YOU GATHER AROUND YOU. MY STORY HAS ALWAYS BEEN ABOUT PEOPLE; MY FAMILY, FRIENDS, CLIENTS, EMPLOYEES, MENTORS AND COACHES.

to do what I did. I like being around people who are smarter than me. It's a way to turn on my brain and come back with ideas I can execute. Even if I only got one good idea, I considered it worth the price of admission.

My life has been blessed by so many wonderful people who have poured into me in so many different ways. I also exercised a certain amount of discernment with the kinds of people I wanted to have around me. Who gives you energy? Who takes away your energy? Who is willing to walk with you? Those are the people I want to spend time with.

The Wall of Gratitude is another idea I stole from Zig Ziglar. It fills a wall in the hallway outside my old office—and it's still there. It's designed to be a list of people that I'm really grateful for who have walked with me since grade school, up to the present. I have a Bible verse at the top and a cross on the side to symbolize my gratitude to Christ for dying on the cross and taking away my sins. Then I have twenty plaques that describe people who have impacted my life; what they did, and how they affected me. They include my parents, my father-in-law, my kids, my wife, a number of customers who I poured into and they opened up to me. There are a couple of school teachers, one from seventh grade, one from when I was a junior in high school. The guy who gave me the first $2,500 loan to buy the business. They are all people who encouraged me along the way, and shared their life with me. It's my way of honoring them and saying thanks. It's also a way of recognizing that I didn't get to where I am all by myself.

That Wall of Gratitude was not only for me. It sends a message to my staff, to my kids, and to anyone who walks by it. It took years to assemble. Cheryln typed them all up and we ordered the frames and assembled them bit by bit.

> NEVER BE AFRAID TO ASK QUESTIONS. FOCUS ON BEING INTERESTED, OVER BEING INTERESTING. BE OPEN AND RECEPTIVE. BE COACHABLE. I THINK YOU WILL FIND THAT PEOPLE ARE MORE THAN WILLING TO POUR INTO THOSE WHO ARE INTERESTED AND ENTHUSIASTIC.

Never be afraid to ask questions. Focus on being interested, over being interesting. Be open and receptive. Be coachable. I think you will find that people are more than willing to pour into those who are interested and enthusiastic.

When you feel yourself getting lost or overwhelmed, go back to what you value. Remember why you're doing what you do. Burn the ships that would take you back to your old thinking and old patterns. Intentional living starts right now. And every day, you are getting one day closer to your someday, whether you choose to or not. So, you might as well start your someday today and begin to *Do Life Big!*

CONCLUSION

AN INVITATION FROM THE AUTHOR

Thank you for taking time and getting this far through my book. Doing life big wasn't just a mantra for Cheryln and myself, it was a way of life, a lifestyle, and a belief system that still fuels everything I do still to this day. So I encourage you to do life big on your own terms.

What does doing life big mean for you?

Take time, think it through, talk to your spouse about it. What does this mean for you? How will you define it? What stories do you want to tell 30 years from today on how you did life big? Live today like the stories you want to tell in the future.

I am here to support you through coaching and mentorship. Please feel free to visit my website.

My website is www.DoLifeBigBook.com. On my website, you can find ways to connect with me as well as learn about things I am up to that I would invite you into with me. This has been a pleasure for me to write and please feel free to reach out to me to share how you are doing life big.

Thank you and I will see you soon!

ABOUT THE AUTHOR

Virg Christoffels is the founder of Christoffels Hair Restoration in Sioux Falls, South Dakota. After four years working as a barber for a leading men's hair styling salon, Virg started his own barber shop in 1976. At the same time, he was losing his hair and began to research replacement options. After starting with very primitive solutions, Virg noticed other businesses that were doing full time hair replacement. In the early 1980's, Virg and his wife Cheryln attended a Zig Zigler seminar where he was exposed to goal setting and business planning. It was then that his dream to have a full-time hair replacement studio in Sioux Falls began. Because he was willing to grow and change, Virg was able to build what is today one of the leading hair loss studios in the world.

Virg and Cheryln worked side by side for forty-four years while raising two children, Sara and Nathan, and eventually becoming grandparents to six grandchildren. Virg found value in developing business systems and challenging his staff to set goals and help build a "team spirit" at work. Virg and Cheryln always worked to have a healthy work/life balance by keeping their faith, family, and play an important part of their life. Making time for family was always a challenge, but they demonstrated that importance by many family trips and hours spent at the lake in the summer. During this time, Virg was also active in leadership roles in his church, school, and community.

Today, their daughter Sara has taken over the business and Virg lives to add value and purpose to himself and other people through coaching, consulting, and mentoring. Virg's works with individuals who are looking to grow or improve a business, or grow and improve themselves. Virg has a gift of listening and then helping clients create goals and become aware of changes that will add value and purpose to their life.

ABOUT THE COMPANY

Christoffels Hair Restoration was founded as a men's barber shop and transformed into one of the world's leading hair loss and hair replacement studios. Beginning with a focus on selling men's hair pieces, Christoffels grew into a business model offering permanent and semi-permanent hair loss solutions, as well as hair loss treatment to both men and women. The pillars that supported the business were, Faith in God, never questioning if it would work, learning to set goals, being surrounded by mentors and coaches, developing a supportive staff through appreciation and quality training, and last but not least... Having a loving wife to help balance all the balls.

Virg was a firm believer in the Dale Carnegie programs, always working with a coach and mentor, and as indicated by his "wall of gratitude," being grateful for those who walk with us through good times and bad. Christoffels is well known for being an award-winning studio raising industry standards, being a visionary in how they developed their business, and sharing that story with other studios. Never being afraid of change and always being deliberate about looking for a better way, Virg was never afraid to call an industry friend, a manufacturer, or a business mentor for advice and encouragement. Virg had the opportunity to teach and train in

Hong Kong and also give numerous presentations at industry gatherings, always being willing to share with his peers. Christoffels adopted the idea that "when the tide comes in, all the boats will rise." It's this attitude that continues to make them leaders in the industry today.